Contents

KT-394-482

A Passion for Paper   **4**
Getting Started
Understanding Paper   6
Collecting and Storing Paper   7
Tools and Equipment   8
Before You Begin   **10**
Essential Techniques   **12**
Perfect Packaging   **16**

Cut Out   20
Punching   **22**
Collage   **26**
Appliqué, Quilting & Embroidery   **28**
Découpage   **32**
Paper Napkin Découpage   **36**
Mix & Match   38

Weave & Fold   40
Weaving   **42**
Lacé®   **44**
Tea Bag Folding   **50**
Iris Folding   **54**
Mizuhiki   **58**
Mix & Match   60

Curl & Coil   62
Quilling   **64**
Mix & Match   72

Relief   74
Parchment Craft   **76**
Prickling   **86**
Embossing   **88**
Mix & Match   92

Printing & Presenting   94
Rubber Stamping   **96**
Scrapbooking   **106**
Mix & Match   110

Three-Dimensional & Motion   112
Paper Sculpture   **114**
Paper Architecture   **116**
Pop-Up   **118**
Mix & Match   124

Templates   126
Suppliers   134
Craft Guilds   135
Glossary / Acknowledgments / About the Author   136
Index   137

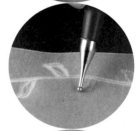

A Passion for Paper

From our earliest years, we display a natural liking for paper – to hold, to read and to create with. Much of paper's irresistible appeal is in its colour, pattern and texture. With the recent proliferation in the variety of paper readily available, papercrafts have boomed in popularity. Traditional papercrafts, such as pricking and weaving, have been revisited and revamped, and in the meantime papercrafts such as rubber stamping and iris folding have emerged.

This book is a fully illustrated, step-by-step guide to papercrafts enjoyed by people all over the globe. Both highly practical and inspirational, it offers a comprehensive range of techniques along with exciting projects to provide the novice papercrafter with a sound foundation on which to progress. In addition, these give the intermediate crafter the opportunity to refresh and hone their skills, and will challenge advanced papercrafters to extend their creative repertoire.

THE PAPER
CRAFTER'S
BIBLE

Elizabeth Moad

David & Charles

A DAVID & CHARLES BOOK
David & Charles is a subsidiary of F&W (UK) Ltd.,
an F&W Publications Inc. company

First published in the UK in 2004

Distributed in North America
by F&W Publications, Inc.
4700 East Galbraith Road
Cincinnati, OH 45236
1-800-289-0963

ISBN 0 7153 1664 8 hardback
ISBN 0 7153 1665 6 paperback

Printed in Singapore by KHL
for David & Charles
Brunel House   Newton Abbot   Devon

Commissioning Editor Fiona Eaton
Editor Jennifer Proverbs
Senior Designer Lisa Forrester
Production Controller Jen Campbell
Project Editor Jo Richardson
Photographer Karl Adamson

Visit our website at www.davidandcharles.co.uk

David & Charles books are available from all good
bookshops; alternatively you can contact our Orderline
on (0)1626 334555 or write to us at FREEPOST
EX2 110, David & Charles Direct, Newton Abbot,
TQ12 4ZZ (no stamp required for UK mainland).

WHAT EXACTLY IS PAPER?

Papyrus was developed by the ancient Egyptians as one of the earliest forms of paper. As the centuries passed, paper making progressed throughout the world and different techniques were adopted in various regions, with the Chinese pulping raw materials, then using a mesh and mould drawn through the pulp to form sheets of paper. The Chinese method gave the fibres of the raw materials a random pattern. In the 18th century, machinery was invented which brought about the mass production of paper, triggering an amazing growth in paper availability, not just for newspapers and books but for crafts such as découpage and quilling. With machine-made paper, the fibres lie in one direction as a result of the manufacturing process, giving it a grain.

WHY PAPERCRAFTS?

With all the fantastic papers that are now available, how can anyone resist getting stuck into papercrafting? You don't have to be a genius to learn these crafts, or be good at drawing or painting to make the projects – enthusiasm is all that's needed. And the only investment required is a few basic tools and your time. The pleasure that you can bring to others who receive your cards and gifts will be greater than you may realize, but the most important factor is your own personal satisfaction. Wonderful, original items can be made in just a short space of time – it doesn't have to take ages to make something for it to be special!

HOW DO I START?

First, decide which of the featured papercrafts appeals to you. You may already have something in mind or you have tried a particular papercraft and want to take it further. But if not, look through the projects in this book and you will soon find something that has particular appeal for you. Whether you are a beginner or more experienced crafter, read through the front of the book where you will discover vital information on everything from paper itself and essential techniques, to creating packaging and organizing your workspace. The next step is to learn the basic technique for your chosen papercraft, and these always appear on a colour-tinted page. Then put your new-found skills into practice by making one of the accompanying projects. For certain papercrafts, there are additional techniques to take it on a creative stage further. Each section of the book features a 'Mix & Match' showcase of cards and other stationery items to illustrate how different techniques can be combined and to offer extra inspiration.

So choose your papers, gather the equipment and start papercrafting today!

Getting Started

The central ethos of this book is that you don't need a vast array of expensive equipment and materials to produce fantastic results. Invest in a few basic but good-quality items from which you can extract the maximum use. Build up your stocks of papers and tools over time, rather than rushing out and buying everything that you think you will need at the start.

The following is a guide to the basic paper, tools and materials you will need for papercrafting. These crop up in many of the techniques and projects featured in the book, where you will also find a 'basic tool kit' and guidance on the appropriate paper to use accompanying each specific technique.

UNDERSTANDING PAPER

Paper for crafters still falls into either the machine-made or handmade category. Each technique featured in the book recommends the type of paper to use for the best results, as does each project, but you will always have the freedom to experiment.

HANDMADE AND MACHINE-MADE

Handmade papers are readily available from exotic places such as Bali, Nepal, India and Thailand. These come in fabulous colours, but it is their different textures and surfaces that set them apart from machine-made papers. Handmade papers often have natural elements like grasses, petals or leaves embedded in them, which makes them much thicker than everyday paper. Embroidered handmade papers are available which offer amazing surfaces for any craft project. Handmade papers generally come in large sheets and are relatively expensive, but a single sheet carefully stored can be used for several projects and so is a good investment.

Machine-made papers should not be over-looked as they can be printed with superb and often quirky designs. These generally come in small sheets and are less expensive than handmade papers. Machine-made papers are also available with textured surfaces, such as embossed or cor-rugated, and so can give a handmade feel to a project. For specialist papercrafts such as quilling or parchment craft, machine-made papers are available in a range of sizes, colours and patterns. Machine-made papers will also go through a home printer, offering an easy, effective way to customize and personalize cards.

GRAIN AND WEIGHT

These are both important features of paper. Like wood, paper has a grain. Working with the grain means that the paper will tear in a relatively straight line. Working against the grain means that it is harder to tear the paper and it will have a much more uneven edge (see page 12).

Paper weight is measured in grams per square metre and is abbreviated to 'gsm' or 'g/m^2'. As a general rule, lightweight paper is everyday stationery paper, such as photocopier paper, and weighs between 80 and 120gsm; medium-weight paper is 120–150gsm; heavyweight paper is 150–250gsm; card is over 250gsm.

COLLECTING AND STORING PAPER

The best approach to getting together the materials you need to practise your papercrafting is to keep on the lookout and build up gradually over time. This is also a more creative and rewarding way of mustering your resources. It is a good idea to shop around – the Internet now gives us greater purchasing power and a wider choice, from suppliers all around the world. You may not want to buy over the Internet but it can allow you to find out more about suppliers and what they have to offer. You may also want to ask your local craft shop if they can order a particular product for you. However, take care not to get too carried away. Think about usefulness and also consider the storage implications.

GATHERING PAPER

Paper is everywhere we look. It is an integral part of our lives, so why do we automatically buy it from a craft shop? Newspapers, magazines, catalogues, labels, stamps, paper napkins, paper handkerchiefs and sheet music are all ideal for papercrafting. Keep on the lookout for different papers. If they are interesting, then you may well be able to use them in a papercraft project.

If you are on holiday and find a special paper, buy several sheets and remember to make a note of the name of the shop or company. There is nothing more frustrating than finding that you only have a tiny piece of a particular paper left and not remembering where it came from. In addition to the Internet, mail order is a good way of sourcing unusual papers.

STORAGE

It is useful to think about storage as you develop as a crafter. It is amazing how quickly you will accumulate all sorts of material. Our loved ones may call it rubbish, but to crafters it is valuable ephemera – a ribbon from a gift, pieces of used or leftover giftwrap, a pretty coloured envelope, a magazine clipping. However, it can all too easily take over. Not everything has to be neat and tidy and everyone works differently, but you need to establish your own system of organizing materials so that you can find what you are looking for.

When it comes to storing paper, temperature is an important factor. Papers can curl and warp in high temperatures, but can become damp and wrinkled in cold conditions. Always store paper out of direct sunlight. Handmade papers come in large sheets, so roll these and store in cardboard tubes if you are short of space, or keep them flat in a portfolio under a sofa or bed. Generally, try to keep papers flat – if they are left standing upright, they will buckle and bend. Keep them out of any danger of being squashed and crumpled. Office filing trays are good for keeping papers in order on your work desk so that they are accessible.

Quilling papers in particular require special storage as they can easily become a tangled mess, bent and squashed. A good idea is to sort the papers by colour or width in a plastic storage container with several drawers.

This plastic storage unit has different-sized drawers. The deeper ones are used to store 1cm (⅜in) wide quilling paper, while the smaller drawers are used for thinner papers.

TOOLS AND EQUIPMENT

If you are starting a new papercraft, buy the minimum amount of tools and equipment that you need – just the essentials. After all, your chosen papercraft may not turn out to be for you after all and you don't want to spend a lot of money on things that you may never use again. However, you will find that one tool can be used for many papercrafts, so you may not need to purchase any new tools to take up another craft.

BASIC TOOL KIT

For any papercraft, it is a good idea to assemble a basic tool kit and keep it organized, well-stocked and to hand.

scissors

★

craft knife

★

metal ruler

★

sharp pencil

★

rubber

★

bone folder

★

PVA (white) glue, dish and cocktail sticks

★

glue stick

★

double-sided adhesive tape

★

low-tack adhesive tape

★

cutting mat

★

scrap paper and card

GLUES

Different types of glues and adhesives are required in papercrafting for particular purposes, so it is important to keep the range in your kit to achieve the best results.

PVA (WHITE) GLUE

This water-based all-purpose glue, which becomes transparent when dry, is suitable for the majority of papercrafts. A small amount can be poured onto a saucer or dish and applied with a cocktail stick for delicate work, but if applied in large quantities to paper, it will make it soggy and wrinkled. It is easy to wash off hands and equipment but, most important-ly, it is the cheapest adhesive.

GLUE STICKS

These are tubes of solid glue that can be rubbed over areas to leave a sticky residue. They are good for applying an even coat of adhesive that won't make the paper soggy. Be sure to replace the lid immediately after use, otherwise the glue stick will dry up.

GLITTER GLUES

These are available in a wide range of colours. They are intended for decorative purposes only, not as conventional glue.

SUPERGLUE

This is useful to keep handy for those instances when it is necessary to ensure a long-lasting adhesion. For example, use superglue for attaching wiggly eyes to cards so that they don't fall off during transit in the mail. This glue is extremely powerful and must be used with extreme care. Keep it well out of reach of children. It will also mark work surfaces.

DOUBLE-SIDED ADHESIVE TAPE

This is a wonderful invention. It is exactly what it says it is – tape that is sticky on both sides. Pieces or lengths are cut and stuck down like ordinary tape, then the backing strip is removed to reveal the adhesive surface. You may prefer to use this rather than PVA (white) glue. Double-sided adhesive tape is ideal for mounting work behind apertures (see page 15).

ADHESIVE FOAM PADS

These are small foam pads that are sticky on both sides, similar to double-sided adhesive tape. However, because they are foam pads, they raise whatever is glued to them away from the surface and so give it a three-dimensional effect. They are available in a block of small pads or individual larger pads.

CUTTING TOOLS

Making a choice of cutting tools is mostly a case of finding what you like to use and feel comfortable with.

SCISSORS

As you develop as a crafter, you will find yourself acquiring several different pairs of scissors. But essentially, you need a large pair for trimming and a small pair for intricate work. Cutting adhesive tape or glued paper can leave a residue on the blades, which may then transfer onto your work, so keep the blades of scissors clean and also sharp.

FANCY-EDGED SCISSORS

These are scissors that have blades ready-cut with a decorative edge so that when the paper is cut, a fancy edge is created. These are good for cutting borders and jazzing up edges.

CRAFT KNIVES

This is the best tool to use for cutting longer straight edges. Some craft knives are durable and some have disposable blades. Always use a craft knife with a metal ruler – the knife can cut nicks in the plastic one, making it unusable. Always use a craft knife on a cutting mat to protect your work surface – it is cheaper to replace a mat than work surfaces. If the craft knife does not have a retractable blade, always stick the blade into a cork to prevent accidents. Replace blades regularly as a blunt blade will not leave a clean cut.

CUTTING MAT

A self-healing cutting mat, such as the green mat shown at the bottom of the page, is essential. When cut with a knife, the edges of the cut come together again, or heal, so as not to leave an indent. It is not only useful when cutting papers with a craft knife but also protects your work surface from glue and scissors. However, the mat will only cope with vertical cuts – angled cuts will gouge out parts.

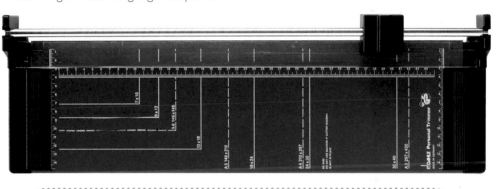

PAPER TRIMMERS

Paper trimmers (below) or guillotines come in a wide variety, from large to small and from cheap to expensive. They are not essential to start with, but if you find that you are frequently cutting with a craft knife, you may wish to invest in one to save time and effort.

STORAGE

Wasting time searching for a particular tool can be frustrating, so you need to keep items accessible but in some order. If you do more than one papercraft, you may prefer to arrange items by craft, for instance all parchment craft tools and equipment could be stored in one box, all quilling tools and equipment in another. Or you may wish to store all tools, such as scissors, together.

When purchasing plastic storage containers, it is a good idea to measure where they are going to go – they may, for instance, slide neatly under your work surface. Store craft books near to your work area for quick reference, or for when you need inspiration.

This three-drawer plastic tool box can be used to store papercrafting tools and equipment.

Before You Begin

Now that you are ready to start papercrafting, here are some important options to consider first to help you gain the most from your creative endeavours. Whether you only plan to spend an hour a day at papercrafts or a whole day, you will need the appropriate work area and working methods. So organize yourself and your surroundings in advance. Also, think about whether you might expand your papercrafting activities in the future. Rather than working in isolation, you may prefer the idea of crafting with other people, perhaps through joining a craft club or guild. Or you may want to develop your expertise to the extent of selling your work. This will all have practical implications.

WORKSPACE

If you don't have a spare room in your house to dedicate to papercrafting, then a corner of a room can easily become a craft zone. With a desk, chair and plastic storage containers, a craft area can be established that is yours and yours alone. Try to set such an area aside for your crafts so that you can sit down at any time and begin without any fuss. Accessibility of equipment has a direct influence on how creative you feel.

With a little ingenuity, it is possible to create a portable workspace. Using plastic storage containers with compartments, tools and papers can be conveyed in a vehicle so that you can craft elsewhere. This is ideal if you are part of a club or have a crafter friend you like to visit.

WORK SURFACE

Any work surface that is flat, clean and of a reasonable size for you to spread out on is ideal. The kitchen or dining room table is fine. Whatever table or desk you are using, check that it is a comfortable height and choose a chair that allows you to sit with your back supported. We take care over these things when working at computers and the same principles apply to your craft workspace.

LIGHTING

Lighting is a factor that is often overlooked because we just don't notice it. But it is the most crucial, since we need to work in a well-lit environment to avoid damaging our eyesight. Special bulbs are available that are blue in colour and aim to provide a natural light. If you enjoy working in miniature or fine detail, it may be worth investing in a magnifying glass. A modest investment in effective lighting will be worth it in the long run.

HEALTH AND SAFETY

Consider your own health and safety before you begin – it's an easy area to overlook, but vital if you are going to enjoy your papercrafting to the full.

FUME AND FIRE HAZARDS

If you are using paint, varnish or sprays, make sure that you use them in a well-ventilated room or outside. Always follow the manufacturer's instructions. Keep sharp tools out of the way of children, especially craft knives and scissors. Don't smoke near flammable substances and don't have naked flames near papers – this includes candles.

Be aware of the potential fire hazard of stocks of paper. Install smoke alarms in your workspace.

REPETITIVE STRAIN INJURY

When you get engrossed in a project time passes very quickly and when you stop you may have hand ache. Take regular breaks and exercise your arms, legs and back by stretching and walking. Stop if your eyes become tired.

TIME MANAGEMENT

If you are not working well, or the paper is not doing what you want it to, it is time for a break. Make a hot drink, phone a friend or do some gardening, but do something different for a few minutes and come back to your work refreshed.

Friends and family may ask you to make a card or item for a special occasion. Don't leave this to the last minute. If you are working in the evenings, your eyes may be tired, or you may just have had a bad day at work and not feel like it. Don't leave it to the night before and avoid making promises that you cannot keep.

Larger projects require time to dry, and while they do so, why not use the opportunity to make a few smaller items, for instance a birthday card or two to build up a stock? It is also fun to have several projects in progress at one time.

JOINING CLUBS AND GUILDS

Papercrafting doesn't have to be a solitary activity. Working alongside other people can offer just the encouragement and support you need when you are embarking on papercrafting or a new technique. Joining a craft club or guild is a good way of meeting like-minded people, to benefit from their skills and experience and to exchange ideas as you develop your own expertise and confidence. Guilds often publish newsletters with advice, projects and suppliers. Craft magazines may also publish details of clubs and guilds. Most have an Internet site, so if you have access to the Internet, do a search. You will find a basic listing of craft guilds and their contact details on page 135.

Often craft shops run clubs or workshops where you can learn new techniques and make friends. Scrapbook enthusiasts regularly meet up in one person's house, turning scrapbooking into a productive social event, which is the secret of its widespread success.

A club can simply be two or more people getting together to craft with each other — all that's needed is a kitchen table and coffee!

SELLING YOUR WORK

You may decide to make your papercrafting a paying hobby by selling your work. There are, however, many things to consider before going down this route. A small, local craft fair is a good starting point for selling your work to the public. But before you book a stand or stall at a craft fair, you need to do some serious groundwork.

GET FEEDBACK Give your work to family and friends for their feedback, but ask them what they liked best – you will soon see patterns developing according to age and gender.

RESEARCH YOUR MARKET Assess the market to which you are selling – visit craft fairs in your area and see at what price other people are selling similar items to yours.

BUDGET Work out how much it costs to produce the item you are selling and take this figure away from the price at which you will sell the item – the difference is the profit per item. Establish how many items you need to sell to cover the costs involved – the stand, packaging, transport costs, and so on – and don't forget to check on the tax implications.

PLAN Plan how your craft stand will look and mock it up at home beforehand – work out how to display your goods to their best advantage. Check with the craft fair organizers what time you can get in on the day to set up and make sure you are arrive early to avoid any last-minute panics.

MAKE Time how long it takes you to make one item, then multiply this by the number of items you need – it can be quite a shock! Ensure that you have enough materials in stock and order in bulk where possible. Get business cards made on which your contact details are printed.

COPYRIGHT

There are many ways to begin selling your work, such as to family and friends, holding parties and supplying to shops and other retail outlets, but it is important to take the copyright implications into consideration in all cases.

It is an offence to use any part of a work, whether it is a book, a design, a painting or an image, if it is protected by copyright. This includes rubber stamps, paper punches, paper napkins, giftwrap and some printed papers. If you want to sell your work, it must be your own original design or you must check out the copyright situation first. Copyright is complex, and if you are in any doubt, find out more before you proceed rather than taking any chances. Bear in mind how misused you would feel if you had spent a long time designing a card and sold it locally, then one day you walk into a store and see your design on sale, and you haven't been acknowledged as the designer and are not receiving any payment for it.

After sending a card through the mail, ask the recipient what state it arrived in. If it was damaged, you will need to either amend your design or your packaging.

Essential Techniques

Although there are excellent card suppliers that offer pre-cut cards of many shapes and sizes, some basic card-crafting skills will come in useful. For instance, you may have a card that you want to use but it does not have an aperture, or you may wish to make something completely unique and cut your own card to size. A handmade card or other item should still look professional. Uneven cutting can really stand out, and if you notice that something is not quite straight, then the recipient will too, so it is best to get it right first time.

SCORING AND FOLDING

Scoring paper allows it to be folded neatly and easily. A crisper fold is created and results in a more professional-looking finish.

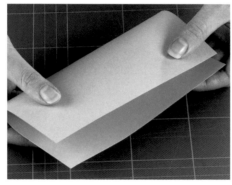

1 Make two pencil marks where you want the score line on the wrong side of the paper and line up the ruler with these marks. Draw an empty ballpoint pen all the way along the line so that the paper is indented. One blade of an open pair of scissors can be used as an alternative. Draw it lightly along the line so that only the topmost fibres of the paper or card are cut. The scored line will become the inside of the fold.

2 Use both hands to fold the paper or card along the score line – it should fold easily.

3 Once the paper or card has been folded, use a bone folder on its side to press along the fold line to make it sharp. The back of a clean metal spoon could be used in place of a bone folder.

TEARING

As an alternative to cutting, a torn edge adds an interesting dimension and can break up an otherwise uniform edge. When tearing paper, you will need to take into account the grain of the paper.

If you are not sure of the grain of a particular paper, test first on a small piece of the paper.

Tearing with the grain
Tearing with the grain is easy and can produce a relatively straight line as the paper naturally wants to tear this way.

Tearing against the grain
Tearing against the grain is harder and produces more uneven tears.

CUTTING

The cleanest cuts are made with a flat, clean surface, a sharp craft knife and metal ruler and a steady hand.

1 Use an HB pencil and a metal ruler to make two pencil marks on the paper where you want the cutting line if you are cutting a small piece, or make three pencil marks if large. With the paper on a cutting mat, place your metal ruler along the line to be cut. It is advisable to stand when cutting with a craft knife so that you can put pressure on the ruler to hold it firmly in place while you draw the knife towards you. Always cut paper so that the section you want to use is under the ruler, then if the knife slips, it will cut into the waste part of the paper.

2 If it is a large sheet, cut approximately 20cm (8in), then, keeping the knife in the paper, move your other hand down the ruler, press firmly down and continue cutting. If it is a very large sheet, you will need to do this several times and using a long metal ruler is essential. With a small sheet of paper, make the cut in a single movement.

3 Keep the blade of the craft knife at a 45-degree angle when cutting. Draw the knife across the paper but don't press too hard or the paper will wrinkle and an uneven edge will be left. When cutting thick paper, draw the blade across once without too much pressure, then again with more pressure to make the final cut.

The metal ruler used here has a non-slip surface attached to the underside, which helps considerably to keep it in place on the paper when cutting or tearing.

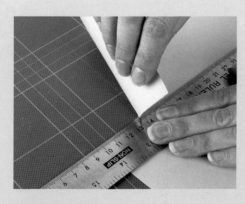 

When using the punch wheel, place the paper on a foam pad, rather than a cutting mat. This allows the paper to 'give' when rolling the tool over it.

Tearing with a ruler
If straight but torn lines are required, use a ruler as a guide. Hold the ruler firmly with one hand and pull the paper up and towards you with the other hand.

Tearing with a punch wheel tool
If you have a punch wheel tool, run this along a ruler to perforate the paper. The paper will then tear easily along the perforation, creating the effect of a postage-stamp edge.

CUTTING AND MOUNTING APERTURES

An aperture refers to the hole cut out of a piece of paper or card. A single-fold or a two-fold card may have an aperture – either in a pre-cut card or one you have cut yourself. The advantage of using a single-fold card with an aperture is that it lets the light through whatever is placed in the aperture. A two-fold card has three panels, with the aperture in the central panel. The third panel is folded over to cover the reverse of the insert.

CUTTING

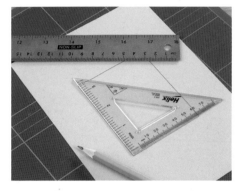

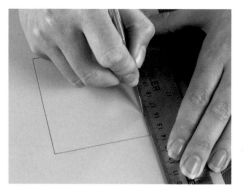

1 Using an HB pencil and ruler, draw the aperture you wish to cut out onto paper or card. Use a set square to ensure that the corners are right angles.

2 Using a sharp craft knife and metal ruler, carefully cut along your first marked line. The ruler should be on the good area of the paper or card so that if the knife slips it cuts into the central portion, which will be removed. Turn the paper round for each cut so that you draw the knife towards you on each cut. Make sure that your cuts don't extend beyond your marked lines.

3 When you have cut all four sides of the aperture, the central portion should fall away. If it does not fall away, use the craft knife to cut the corners carefully so that it falls away. Do not pull it out or you will tear or damage the corners.

MOUNTING

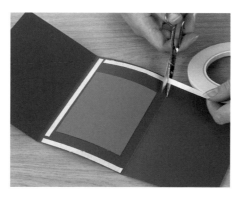

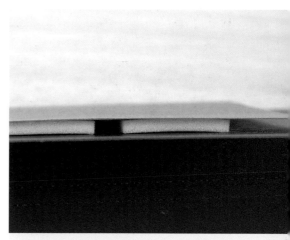

1 To mount a paper panel into an aperture, ensure that it is at least 1cm (⅜in) larger than the aperture. Place lengths of double-sided adhesive tape around the aperture window on the inside of the card – a two-fold card has been used here. Remove the backing from the tape and place the insert, right-side down, onto the tape, then press down firmly. You may find it easier to position the paper by turning the card over so that you can see the right side and holding it over the work you want to insert in order to position it correctly.

2 When the insert has been mounted in the aperture, turn the card right-side down and place lengths of double-sided adhesive tape along the four edges of the central panel of the card. Remove the backing and fold the third panel over the wrong side of the insert. Press firmly so that all parts are firmly stuck down. You now have a single-fold card. Double-sided adhesive tape does not allow you to reposition the insert. Glue – either a glue stick or PVA (white) glue – can be used instead and will allow you to move it slightly if positioned incorrectly.

An alternative technique is to use adhesive foam pads to mount paper onto a card. These are sticky on both sides of a foam core and have the effect of lifting the image from its background, adding depth.

From left to right: These first four stationery items (Glitzy Gift Tags, page 43, Vintage Celebration, 92, Fern Panels, page 87 and Sartorial Stationery, page 61) demonstrate the use of different apertures, while the final project (Messages from the Heart, page 60) is an example of using adhesive foam pads for mounting.

Perfect Packaging

Presentation and packaging is important, since it can complement and therefore enhance your work. Making envelopes, boxes and bags will not only impress the recipient but give extra protection through the mail or any other method of delivery. If, on the other hand, you are selling your work, poor presentation will result in low sales.

The techniques that follow show you how to make basic items of packaging, which can be made to fit any size of item, and the gift bag will encompass any shape. These can be customized or coordinated with the card or gift it contains, and you could also add additional features, such as a matching gift tag or label. Once you have mastered the basics, you may want to move on to create some of the more adventurous designs featured in the book, like the examples below.

ENVELOPE

If you have taken time to make a card, then spend just a few more minutes to make an envelope. If you don't have a ready-made envelope to fit your handmade card, it is far better to tailor-make one than to use a bought envelope that is too big for the card. Use paper that is strong yet will fold neatly.

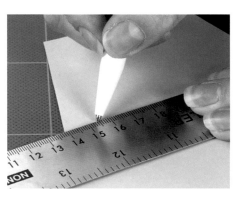

1 Photocopy the template on page 127 and cut out, then draw around the template onto scrap card to make your own template which you can then keep and use as many times as you need. Draw around your card template onto your chosen paper. Cut out the envelope with scissors.

2 Place the envelope right-side down on a cutting mat. Using an empty ballpoint pen against a metal ruler, score along the dashed lines across the flaps marked on the template.

3 Use a glue stick to run a line of glue along the two side edges of one of the larger flaps. Fold the two smaller side flaps inwards and press the glued flap onto these.

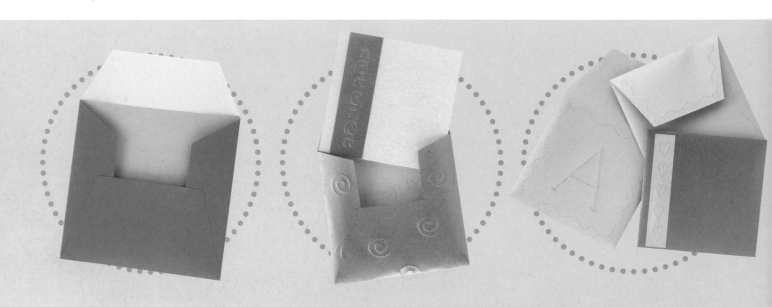

This gift bag can be used in its simplest form, as shown here, or you can add handles. Do this by cutting or punching holes in the paper and threading cord through, or cutting holes large enough for a hand to fit through.

GIFT BAG

Paper gift bags are quick and easy to make. They can be made in any size and are ideal packaging for awkward-shaped gifts. Medium-weight paper should be used and good-quality giftwrap is perfect for the job. Thin paper can be used if it is glued to stronger paper.

The size of your bag will be determined by the temporary mould you use to fold around – in this case a small box file, but you could also use a book or an empty box. Cut a sheet of paper long enough to wrap around your box, allowing a generous overlap of approximately 10cm (4in). Decide how tall you want the bag to be and add an extra 6cm (2⅜in) to the height when cutting out the paper.

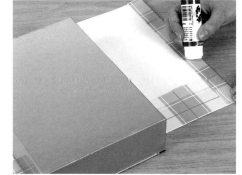

1 Fold over and, using a glue stick, glue 6cm (2⅜in) along the top long edge of the paper. Fold over and glue 6cm (2⅜in) along one of the short edges. Place the box you are using as a temporary mould in the centre of the paper. Glue along the folded short edge.

2 Wrap the paper around the box so that the two short edges overlap and making sure that the folded edge is uppermost. Also make sure that the folded edges are level at the top of the bag. Press firmly down to stick.

3 For the base of the bag, neatly fold over the end flaps as if you are wrapping a present. Glue the end flap in place with a glue stick and remove the box. You may now want to push the sides of the bag inwards, pinching the two top edges together.

From left to right:
The finished, plain envelope, then examples of embellished envelopes – Classical Wedding Stationery, page 91, and Personally Presented, page 93. Two examples of the basic gift bag in different forms with additional decorative features – Flower Power Gift Bag, page 27, and Enscrolled Gift Bag, page 125.

GIFT BOX

Gift boxes are a little more time-consuming to make but they are sturdier than gift bags. It is best to make a box to package delicate items. Strong paper or card can be used for gift boxes.

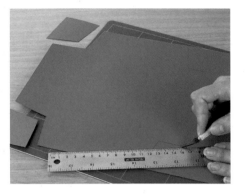
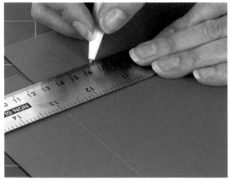

1 Enlarge the template on page 126 on a photocopier by 50% and cut out along the outside solid lines. Draw around the template onto scrap card and cut out using a craft knife and metal ruler. Draw around the card template onto your chosen paper or card and cut out in the same way.

2 Place the box right-side down on a cutting mat. Using an empty ballpoint pen against a metal ruler, score along the dashed lines marked on the template.

3 Using a glue stick, apply glue to the right side of the four tabs on the box base. Press these tabs to the inside of the box sides to form the box base. The lid of the box will then fit neatly into the base.

The template for the gift box can easily be changed in size, or its relative dimensions altered, for instance to make a deeper box.

Left to right:
Both these impressive designs are made using the basic gift box template and instructions given here. For the left-hand box, see Lotus Flower Gift Box, page 115, and for the right-hand box, see Silver-Leaf Gift Box, page 111.

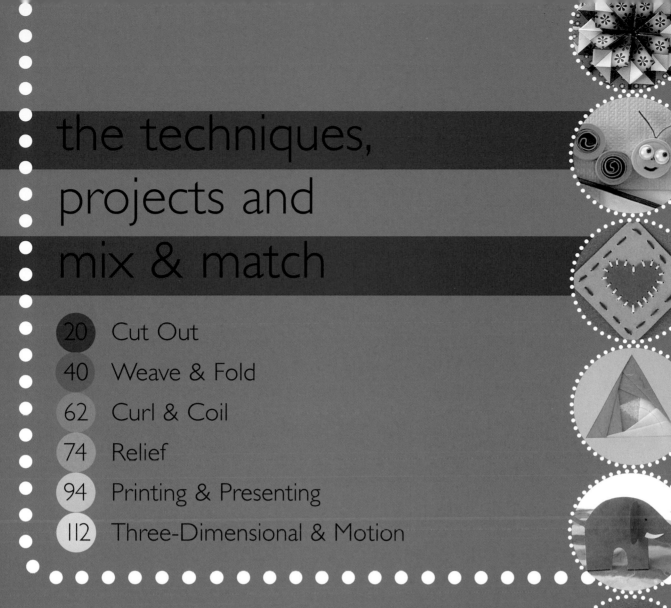

the techniques, projects and mix & match

20 Cut Out

40 Weave & Fold

62 Curl & Coil

74 Relief

94 Printing & Presenting

112 Three-Dimensional & Motion

Cut Out

PUNCHING • COLLAGE • APPLIQUÉ, QUILTING & EMBROIDERY
DÉCOUPAGE • PAPER NAPKIN DÉCOUPAGE

To cut out and arrange paper would seem one of the simplest forms of papercraft, yet it requires an eye for harmony. In punching, you can achieve a pleasing balance by building up repeat patterns, while in collage, the challenge is to create an overall symmetry with a variety of colours, textures and printed patterns. Exploring combinations of different papers, layered one upon another, is the appeal and skill of appliqué, especially in conjunction with embroidery, used to join all the elements together. Découpage demands extra design and compositional abilities when applying printed images to an object, where its shape and use are additional considerations.

Here, you will be guided through the papercrafts, from punching — perfect for beginners as the motifs come preformed — and ending with the more complex découpage. But in Mix & Match, see just how stunning the effects of all these easy-to-master cut-out crafts can be when used together with other papercrafts.

Clockwise from left: Flower Power Gift Bag, page 27; Apple Mosaic Card, page 23; Petal Notelets, page 25; Garden Lover's Gift Tags, page 37; Cupid Keepsake Box, pages 34–35

Punching

The principle of craft punching is the same as with the classic office hole punch, where a metal cutter punches out a paper shape in a single action. The cutter comes in a wide range of sizes and shapes, and just a few are shown here. Paper punches are popular because they are a quick way of making basic, identical shapes, but that is just one simple application. By using different papers and combining it with other papercrafts, the versatility and creative potential of punching will soon become apparent.

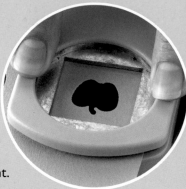

Basic Tool Kit

MOTIF PUNCHES

The heart and train punches are examples of two smaller motif punches, while the apple punch used in the project opposite creates a larger cutout shape – this is a 2.5cm (1in) punch. They all operate in the same way as a regular punch.

SQUARE PUNCHES

Regular-shaped punches such as these two square punches – large and small – are a useful addition to your tool box.

REGULAR HOLE PUNCH

Paper can move freely in the punch slots, allowing you to position it correctly.

CORNER PUNCH

With corner punches, the plastic inserts inside guide the paper so that the punch is cut on the corner every time. These plastic inserts can be removed to allow free movement of the paper as in regular punches.

BORDER PUNCH

A border punch has a pattern that allows it to be repeated to form a punched-out border. They are superb for making the edge of a card or mount look extra special.

Papers

Punches are generally made of metal and can cope with heavy paper but not card. Thin paper and handmade paper may not cut cleanly. If you wish to punch vellum, place a thin sheet of paper under the vellum and punch both together. Punches are a brilliant way of using up those miscellaneous scraps of paper that we all acquire and cannot bear to throw away!

Basic Technique

Punches are easy to use, but with a little imagination, they have many creative possibilities. The shape that is punched out can be used as the main feature of a card or to embellish a design.

PUNCH CARE

If punches are used very frequently, they may need oiling to continue to punch smoothly. Make sure that all excess oil is cleaned from the punch before it is used again.

BASIC PUNCHING

Slide the paper into the punch and place on a hard surface. Apply firm downward pressure to the punch using your fingers or the palm of your hand. Don't just discard the shape that is punched out of the paper. This 'negative' or cutout can also be used.

POSITIONING

By placing the punch upside down, with the cutter uppermost, you are able to position your paper accurately in the punch. Some punches have removable plastic covers on the bottom to catch punched pieces – remove this to see where you are placing the paper.

Project Apple Mosaic Card

Punches are excellent for making cards that appear more time-consuming than they really are. Here, an apple punch and a square punch are used to create an eye-catching greetings card, but the same project would be equally effective with other motif punches you may have, such as a heart or flower.

You will need

foam pad
★
apple punch
★
green paper in light and dark shades
10 x 20cm (1 x 8in)
★
ruler
★
pencil
★
square punch
★
PVA (white) glue
★
cocktail stick
★
stone single-fold card
13cm (5in) square

1 Working over a foam pad to protect your work surface and to prevent slipping, use the apple punch to punch a row of three apple shapes from the light green paper, leaving a space of 4cm (1½in) between each apple. Repeat with the dark green paper. Put all six cutout apple shapes to one side.

2 Take the square punch and place it upside down on your work surface. Slide the punched light green paper into the square punch so that a punched-out apple is positioned centrally in the square. Press down firmly on the punch to punch out the square shape. Repeat with the remaining punched-out apples.

3 Applying the glue with a cocktail stick, glue the six squares with the punched-out apples, alternating the two shades of green, onto the single-fold card, leaving a border of 2cm (¾in) from the top of the card and about 5mm (³⁄₁₆in) in between each square. Glue the cutout apple shapes inside the punched-out apple shapes so that they meet edge to edge, again alternating the two shades to create a contrast.

Make sure your work surface is firm and steady when punching as some punches are quite stiff. You may need to stand up when punching to apply more pressure to the punch.

Further Techniques Creating with Punches

A single punch can be applied in a variety of different ways, making it highly versatile and great value for money. The cutout shapes resulting from the punched design can also be modified to create different effects. Experiment with these further techniques on scrap paper to see how much more you can get out of your existing punches.

MOVING PUNCHES

You can punch a rectangular shape using a square punch simply by punching once, then moving the punch along and punching again. You will need to make sure that there is a slight overlap and that the edges line up exactly. The punch could be moved along several times to create an elongated shape.

LAYERING CUTOUT SHAPES

Using two sizes of heart punch, you can layer different colours on top of each other for a striking effect. Punch one large heart in a colour of your choice, then punch a smaller heart in a complementary colour. Glue the smaller heart cutout on top of the larger heart. Squares could also be layered in the same way, or use two different shapes for layering, as long as one is smaller than the other – for example, a swirl layered on a square or a heart on a square (see the Heart Trio Bookmark project on page 30).

RESHAPING CUTOUT SHAPES

The cutout shapes can be cut or trimmed to make a new shape. Here, small square cutouts were cut in half to make triangles. This is a quick way to make lots of triangles exactly the same without having to measure them out. The Petal Notelets project opposite features this technique, where heart cutouts are cut in half to create petals.

USING THE CORRECT PUNCH
Not all punches can be used for these techniques – for instance, you can't use border or corner punches for reshaping. However, you could use the 'negative' pieces from these punches for layering. For example, tiny fleurs-de-lys from a corner punch were used in the Ideal Home card on page 39.

Petal Notelets

The design for these notelets is created by using cutout shapes from a heart punch cut in half to form a petal and flower pattern. This same principle can be applied to other kinds of motif punches.

You will need

blue notepaper
30 x 21cm (12 x 8¼in)
★
heart punch
★
purple paper in dark and light shades
★
scissors
★
PVA (white) glue
★
cocktail stick
★
regular hole punch

When punching fine paper, place it in the punch with a sheet of scrap paper and punch both together, then discard the scrap paper shape.

1 Take the sheet of blue notepaper and fold it lengthways in half, then in half again so that you have a notelet. Punch out six heart shapes from each of the two purple papers. With a pair of scissors, cut each heart in half down the middle to create petals.

2 Applying the glue with a cocktail stick, glue four dark purple petals to the bottom left-hand corner of the notelet, making sure that they are evenly spaced. Glue four light purple petals in between and slightly overlapping the dark purple petals.

3 Using a hole punch, punch out a circle of dark purple paper. Attach this to the centre of the flower. Make another flower in the opposite corner of the folded notelet in the same way, but start with the light purple petals first and punch out a light purple circle for the centre. With the remaining four petals of each shade, create a border linking the two flowers, again alternating the two shades.

Collage

Paper collage involves arranging different pieces of paper together to make an overall picture or pattern. The word collage comes from 'coller', meaning to gum or glue, and it really is just a matter of gluing paper to paper. Paper collage is often thought of as a children's craft but it is a favourite of significant artists. Its apparent simplicity belies its inherent challenge, to harmonize successfully a jumble of elements into a balanced composition. The papers can be cut, punched or torn into pieces, and while they are traditionally glued in place, they could be sewn. Layers can be built up to create a complexity of surfaces and textures.

Basic Tool Kit

SCISSORS
The size and type of scissors depends on the thickness and type of paper you are cutting.

PUNCH WHEEL TOOL
This is best used on light- or medium-weight paper to create a perforated edge, like a postage stamp. It will not work on fibrous handmade paper.

ADHESIVES
Use either PVA (white) glue, applied with a cocktail stick, or a glue stick for gluing the papers in place.

PAINTBRUSH
For large areas, apply PVA (white) glue with a paintbrush for speed and a more even coverage. If the glue is too stiff, pour some into a dish and add a tiny amount of water to loosen it, but not too much, otherwise it will become too runny.

Papers

The fundamental principle of collage is that you can use paper of any size, shape, colour or thickness, including printed or handwritten paper, such as magazines, bus tickets and shopping lists. Collage can be an economical papercraft as all the waste pieces of paper that are normally thrown away can be used to make surprisingly interesting images. For a specific project, you may wish to purchase coloured paper or colour your own papers using watercolours.

Basic Technique

Collage is an anomaly in papercrafts since it has no specific technique – the only rule involved is that there are no rules. It is the freedom to cut, tear, punch out or use paper materials just as they come that gives collage its unique qualities. However, composition is central to collage, so it is a good idea to lay out your selected elements first. If the overall effect is not balanced, then items can be moved around, added or removed to achieve the final arrangement. Don't be afraid to overlay papers and to build up layers of colour. Papers can be glued or sewn together to provide a background for another image.

Flower Power Gift Bag

A collage of bright, stylized flowers adds a burst of colour to this gift bag, and the matching gift tag finishes off the stylish effect.

Keep the flower templates in a folder so that you have them ready for use in another project.

1 Make your own card templates from the two flower templates on page 128 (see Step 1, page 16). Using a pencil, draw around the large flower template onto one shade of orange paper and cut out. Repeat with the other orange paper, yellow paper and corrugated card. Use the smaller flower template to cut out three flowers from the red and three from the coral paper.

2 Using the hole punch, punch out lots of small circles from the red, coral and yellow papers. Because the red paper was not easy to punch cleanly, it was punched here with the yellow paper.

You will need
scissors
★
pencil
★
scrap card
★
orange paper in dark and light shades, yellow paper and orange corrugated card, each 14 x 15cm (5½ x 6in)
★
red and coral handmade papers 20 x 15cm (8 x 6in)
★
regular hole punch
★
orange and coral gift bag 20 x 33 x 8cm (8 x 13 x 3¼in) (see page 17 for instructions, using an empty cereal box as a mould and a square punch to cut the handles)
★
PVA (white) glue
★
cocktail stick
★
orange paper yarn 40cm (15¾in) long
★
adhesive tape

3 Applying the glue with a cocktail stick, glue the large flowers to the bag first, then glue the smaller flowers to them, alternating the colours. Glue about 10 small punched circles to the centre of each flower – these can overlap and stick out for a textured effect. Cut four more smaller flowers from coral paper and glue to the bag in between the large flowers. Make the tag in the same way as the large flowers. Punch a hole at the top, thread through the yarn and tie or tape to the bag.

Appliqué, Quilting & Embroidery

The word appliqué, from the French, means 'applied'. More usually done with fabric, paper appliqué involves arranging papers, as in collage, and then sewing them together. Paper quilting and embroidery also work in a similar way to their fabric equivalents, and the combination of these techniques offers limitless creative potential and fantastic colour and textural effects.

   As with fabric quilting, papers can be selected and coordinated, then simply cut and glued together to produce dynamic patchwork effects, even incorporating old magazine cuttings and left-over paper scraps as you would remnants of clothing. Paper embroidery can use both cotton and embroidery threads, and different stitches will give paper a unique quality and texture.

Basic Tool Kit

NEEDLES
The needle you require will depend on what you are sewing. Cotton thread requires a fine needle but embroidery needles are needed if you are using embroidery threads.

COTTON AND EMBROIDERY THREADS
These come in many colours and are available from craft or haberdashery shops or suppliers.

PAPER YARN
A cross between thread and string, this is paper twisted into long strands. It is quite stiff but creates interesting textures.

NEEDLE AND CORK
Before stitching, you will need to prick holes in the paper with a needle mounted in a dense cork – a fine needle if you will be sewing with cotton or a larger needle for paper yarn.

FOAM PAD
If pricking holes in paper, you will need a foam pad to work over. It not only protects your work surface but it allows the paper to give a little, making pricking easier.

Papers

Any paper can be sewn. Fine papers may need to be glued to a stronger paper to make them easier to sew. Card should not be used as it is not flexible enough.

Basic Technique

1 To prick out the holes prior to sewing, place your paper over a foam pad and, using the needle mounted in the cork, prick holes where you want the design to be. You may want to have the design on a sheet of tracing paper and prick through this to the paper underneath.

2 Secure the end of the cotton or thread on the wrong side of the paper using adhesive tape, then hand sew using the pricked holes. When you have finished stitching, secure the other end of the thread with tape on the wrong side of the paper.

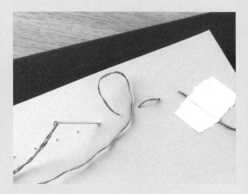

Project Home Sweet Home Card

This patchwork house is a bright and cheerful way to welcome somebody to a new home. Here, a yellow and blue colour scheme has been used, but it could be adapted to whatever papers you have or the recipient's favourite colours. Quilting principles are used, but as there is no stitching involved, it is a quick make.

You will need

small square punch (optional)

★

blue patterned papers

★

scissors

★

PVA (white) glue

★

cocktail stick

★

yellow card
9 x 11 cm (3½ x 4¼in)

★

plain blue card

★

single-fold blue card
14 x 12.5cm (5½ x 4⅞in),
covered with textured indigo
mulberry paper

1 Using a small square punch, punch out 13 squares from the blue patterned papers, or use scissors to cut them 1.6cm (⅝in) square. Using a cocktail stick to apply the glue, glue to the yellow card in three rows of three squares, with no gaps between the squares, to form one larger square.

2 Cut a triangle for the roof from plain blue card 5.5cm (2¼in) long x 3cm (1⅛in) high and glue this just above the square. Cut a rectangle 5 x 2cm (2 x ¾in) for the chimney from blue patterned paper and glue to the right-hand side of the roof. Mount the yellow card to the centre of the single-fold blue card with glue.

3 Glue the four remaining squares to each of the corners of the single-fold card.

Several different patterned squares can be cut from one piece of checked paper. Use scissors or a punch to cut with the lines and then change the angle to cut across the lines.

Project Heart Trio Bookmark

Paper appliqué is a wonderful way of combining scraps of paper to make unusual colour and texture compositions. This bookmark could be placed into a book of love poems for a special Valentine's gift.

This project could be adapted by using a different motif in place of the heart, such as a punched apple or star shape.

You will need

scissors

★

square punch (optional)

★

dark pink and light pink papers

★

heart punch (optional)

★

pink checked paper

★

glue stick

★

foam pad

★

needle and cork

★

embroidery needle

★

light pink, dark pink and cream
embroidery threads

★

adhesive tape

★

dark blue paper
18.5 x 5cm (7⅜ x 2in)

★

double-sided adhesive tape

★

light blue paper
20.5 x 6cm (8 x 2⅜in)

★

regular hole punch

★

dark pink tassel

1 Cut out or punch two 3.5cm (1⅜in) squares from dark pink paper and one square from light pink paper. Cut out, using the template on page 128, or punch two heart shapes from pink checked paper and one from dark pink paper. Glue the checked hearts to the centre of the dark pink squares so that the point of the heart aligns with a corner of the square. Glue the dark pink heart to the light pink square.

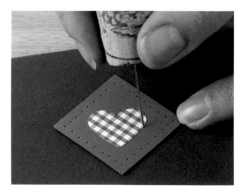

2 Place a dark pink square over a foam pad. Using the needle and cork, prick a border of evenly spaced holes around the edge of the square and then around the heart. Work on the right side as then the displaced paper is on the wrong side.

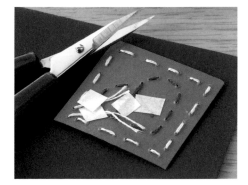

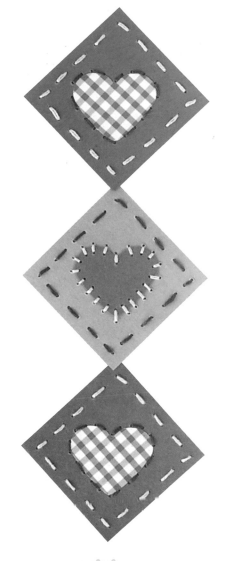

3 Thread an embroidery needle with two strands of light pink embroidery thread. Securing the threads ends with adhesive tape and starting from the wrong side, sew through the holes around the square edge. Using two strands of dark pink embroidery thread, sew around the heart. It does not matter if the wrong side looks untidy. Repeat with the other dark pink square.

4 Prick holes around the edge of the light pink square as before and around the heart, but also prick holes around the inside of the heart opposite the outer holes. Using two strands of dark pink embroidery thread, sew around the square edge. Using two strands of light pink embroidery thread, sew around the heart, sewing from the outer to the inner holes.

5 Prick a row of three x four grouped holes along the top and bottom of the dark blue paper. Using two strands of dark pink embroidery thread, sew a cross in each group of holes.

6 Using double-sided adhesive tape, attach the heart squares to the dark blue paper, overlapping them slightly, then attach the dark blue paper to the light blue paper. Punch a hole in the top of the light blue paper with a hole punch and thread the tassel through.

One of these appliquéd squares mounted onto a single-fold card would make a perfect design for a teenage girl.

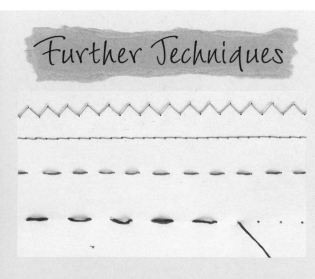

Further Techniques

Expand your repertoire of stitches for different effects. Here are a few ideas to get you started.

Machine stitching
These two rows are machine stitched. Sewing machines are good for making regular stitches if you are not a confident sewer or if you want to sew a large area quickly. Adjust the tension and practise on scrap paper.

Hand stitching with embroidery thread
This row is hand stitched with two strands of embroidery thread. Close up the holes made by the needle around the thread with your finger.

Hand stitching with paper yarn
This row is hand stitched with paper yarn, which is stiff enough to thread through holes without using a needle but needs to be secured on the wrong side with tape. When pricking the holes, use a needle large enough for the yarn to pass through.

Découpage

From the French word 'découper', meaning to cut out, découpage is the craft of cutting out pre-printed pictures, arranging them in a new design and gluing them to an object. Many coats of varnish – sometimes as much as thirty to forty layers – are then applied so that the edges of the paper cutouts disappear under a smooth sheen and the design looks as if it was painted onto the object. As far back as the 12th century, Chinese peasants were sticking paper cutouts to various objects. However, it is the late 17th-century Oriental lacquer work, mainly furniture, that we tend to associate with traditional découpage.

The attraction of this craft is that it can transform old or everyday objects, from cardboard boxes or metal and terracotta items to wooden furniture such as desks or chairs into beautiful ornaments. You can select a découpage project to fit your available time – a simple découpage box can be made in hours, but an item of furniture will take several days. Découpage can also be done in stages, some each day, so that you can work it around other craft projects.

Basic Tool Kit

SANDPAPER

Sandpaper is needed to prepare wooden surfaces prior to decorating. Several grades of sandpaper may be required depending on the state of the wood to begin with. Coarse sandpaper is used first to remove the roughest areas, then a fine grade of sandpaper is used for a smooth finish.

VARNISH

Clear matt or gloss varnish is most commonly used, but there is nothing to stop you from using coloured varnishes or crackle varnish to provide interesting effects.

CLOTH

A damp cloth is required to wipe away excess glue, but make sure that it isn't hairy or fibrous, otherwise it will leave behind material that will get into the varnish.

PAINTBRUSHES

The size of brush you need depends on what size project you are undertaking, so a large box is going to require a large brush. Use good-quality brushes as they are less likely to shed hairs. Several brushes will be required as it is best to keep one for paint, one for glue and one for varnish.

GLUE

Use PVA (white) glue for découpage, applied with a paintbrush, since it dries quickly. It can be watered down a little to make spreading over large areas easier.

Papers

All sorts of papers can be used for this craft. Colour or black and white photocopies of photographs, giftwrap or magazines can be used. Old-fashioned scraps are still being printed and can be bought in sheets where the design is cut out and held in place with small tabs so that with only a little trimming they are ready to use.

Basic Technique

Read the key stages of découpage, below, then take time to practise the basic technique before you embark on the project.

Key Stages

Although découpage is an amazingly simple papercraft, taking time to master the following key stages will ensure professional-looking and long-lasting results.

PREPARING THE SURFACE

A smooth, clean surface is vital. If you are using a new object such as a wooden photo frame or box, a light rub with fine sandpaper is all that is needed. If you are using an old or second-hand piece of furniture, this is likely to require more sanding. Metal objects must have any rust removed with a wire brush and then be painted with a metal primer. Pottery must be sealed with a water-based varnish. Glass surfaces must be clean.

CUTTING AND COMPOSING

Cutting out can be fiddly and time-consuming depending on what images are used. It is recommended that both sides of the paper are coated with a sealant such as Shellac before they are cut out. This is an optional step and depends on what you are making and how many years you want it to last. Once you have cut out all the images for your design, try out the composition first by positioning the paper cutouts with reusable pliable adhesive before gluing in place.

VARNISHING

Traditionally, many layers of varnish are applied to the object for protection, so time has to be allowed for each layer to dry. The number of coats needed depends on how thick the paper cutouts are and how hard-wearing you want the object to be. But remember that the edges of the paper cutouts should not be detectable, so apply a minimum of three coats of varnish. Apply varnish in a well-ventilated and dust-free room with a good-quality brush and leave to dry thoroughly.

1 Cut out the design you want to use with a small pair of scissors. Take care when cutting detailed and intricate edges.

2 Using a brush, coat the back of the cutout with a thin layer of PVA (white) glue, ensuring an even coverage all over – pay particular attention to the edges.

3 Place the cutout onto the object glue-side down. Using a damp clean cloth, smooth out any wrinkles, working from the centre of the cutout to the edges. Press down so that the cutout is firmly adhered and wipe away any excess glue. The cutout is fragile at this stage and will tear easily. Glue on all the remaining cutouts in this way and leave to dry. If any papers curl up, use a cocktail stick to apply more glue to the area, press down and leave to dry.

4 When the glue has completely dried, apply a coat of varnish to the whole object. It is better to apply several thin coats of varnish than one thick coat.

PRECISION HANDLING

Use a pair of tweezers to pick up and position small pieces of glued paper for a clean, precise finish.

Project Cupid Keepsake Box

This plain wooden box is transformed with découpage into a delightful keepsake. The lid of the box is decorated with flower garlands and cupids, with smaller cupids on all four sides of the base of the box. Cupids have a timeless, enduring quality, giving the box a traditional feel while still being very much in vogue.

You will need

MDF wooden box with lid
7.5 x 15 x 10cm (3 x 6 x 4in)
★
newspaper
★
fine-grade sandpaper
★
cream emulsion paint
★
paintbrushes
★
paper scraps –
two large cupids, four smaller cupids,
flower border 48cm (19in) long
and two floral corners
★
small scissors
★
reusable pliable adhesive
★
PVA (white) glue
★
damp cloth
★
gloss or matt varnish

1 Place the box and lid on newspaper and sand with fine-grade sandpaper. Wipe to remove any excess dust.

After painting the box, check that the lid still fits — the inside rim may need light sandpapering to remove excess paint.

2 Paint the whole box inside and out with cream emulsion paint and leave to dry. It will need three coats of paint to give the box an even colour.

3 Cut out all the cupid and flower shapes using small scissors.

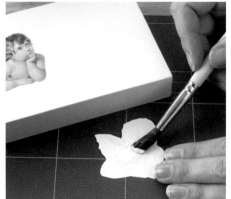

4 Using reusable pliable adhesive, arrange all the shapes on the box – two large cupids on the lid and two flower corners in opposite corners; one smaller cupid on each side of the box; lengths of flower border on each side of the lid. This ensures that the shapes are of the correct size and in the right position before gluing.

5 Take one large cupid off the box and remove the reusable pliable adhesive. Using a paintbrush, coat the back of the cutout with glue.

Varnish in a dust–free environment away from draughts, otherwise bits of fluff will get onto your varnished surface and spoil it.

6 Place the cupid in position on the box lid. Using a damp cloth, press the shape down onto the lid and wipe away any excess glue. Glue all the shapes onto the box in the same way and leave to dry.

7 Working in a well-ventilated space, apply three coats of varnish to the box and lid, leaving to dry thoroughly between each coat.

Another cupid or some additional flowers could be glued inside the lid of the box for added decorative interest.

Paper Napkin Découpage

A contemporary twist on traditional découpage, this is exactly what it says it is – découpage using paper napkins. Paper napkins are widely available from supermarkets and department stores, inexpensive and come in packs of multiples, so if a design does not turn out right first time, there are plenty more images you can use. Paper napkin découpage is suitable for greetings cards or gift tags, but it can also be used for decorating wooden or ceramic items.

Papers

While paper napkin découpage uses three-ply napkins, only the top layer of the ply, which is printed, is actually required. The advantage of using such a fine paper is that there is no raised edge, as there is with the thicker paper used in traditional découpage.

Basic Tool Kit

PVA (WHITE) GLUE AND PAINTBRUSH

PVA (white) glue dries quickly and can be watered down a little to make spreading over large areas easier. Use a paintbrush to apply a thin, even layer of glue to the surface or object to be decorated. The size of brush required will depend on the area to be covered.

SCISSORS

You will need a good-quality, sharp pair of scissors with fine-pointed blades for cutting out motifs or designs from the napkins when applying to an object (see Basic Technique).

Basic Technique

1 Separate the top ply only of the napkin to be used. This is a very fine gossamer paper which is easily torn, so be sure to handle it with great care.

2 In paper napkin découpage, glue is applied to the surface to be decorated rather than the image. If working onto paper or card, use a brush to apply a thin, even layer of PVA (white) glue to the right side, covering enough to take the whole of the printed napkin design.

APPLYING A SINGLE IMAGE

When applying to an object, it is easier to cut out the image from the napkin before separating the layers of ply. Apply glue to the surface of the object, then gently lower the image onto the glued surface. Don't worry if part of the image is on the edge of the napkin with a slightly raised pattern, as this will flatten out when glued.

3 Lower the napkin paper, print-side up, onto the glued paper or card, gradually laying it down from one corner to another to avoid trapping air bubbles. Take great care as the paper is very fragile at this stage. Use your fingers to gently smooth out any wrinkles. Leave to dry, then cut out the image or images using scissors.

Project Garden Lover's Gift Tags

These gift tags are great for gardening presents and are really quick to make. Here, several tags were made from a single paper napkin.

You will need

paper napkin with gardening motifs
★
paintbrush
★
PVA (white) glue
★
cream card
21 x 30cm (8¼ x 12in)
★
scissors
★
regular hole punch
★
lengths of mizuhiki cord,
for the ties

If you don't remove the other ply layers, they will absorb the glue and the top layer with the design will not adhere properly to the surface.

1 Separate the top printed ply of the napkin and discard the other layers. Using a paintbrush, apply a thin, even layer of glue to the card, ensuring that a large enough area is covered so that every part of the design can be stuck down.

2 Lower the napkin paper print-side up onto the glued card. Once in position, gently smooth out the wrinkles with clean, dry fingers, working from the centre outwards. However, do not over-handle the work. Leave to dry.

3 Using scissors, cut out the motifs in a gift tag shape. With this particular paper napkin, the motifs were already framed within a printed gift tag, so they were simply cut out following the tag outlines. Punch a hole in the top of each tag, thread a length of mizuhiki cord through and knot to secure.

You can use printed paper handkerchiefs for découpage in the same way as paper napkins — see the Hello Baby! card on page 38 as an example.

Mix & Match

3-D Bugs

This card features a combination of collage and quilling (see pages 64–65). The ladybird's spots were punched with a regular hole punch, while the caterpillar was made of coils of 3mm (⅛in) wide quilling paper. The veins of the leaves were lightly scored with scissors. A butterfly could be featured in place of the ladybird, such as the ones in the Butterfly Hover card on page 124, but attached to the card rather than a pop-up.

Hello Baby!

A suitably delicate touch is brought to this card for a new baby or a christening with the use of a paper handkerchief, as in paper napkin découpage. The border features a pricked design from a metal stencil (see pages 86–87), which was worked from the front so that the raised edges are inwards. The card colour could be changed to pink for a girl.

Apple Embroidery

An ordinary writing pad is transformed with a handcrafted cover. Apple shapes were punched, attached to mulberry paper and then outlined with hand stitching in cotton. Mizuhiki cord was threaded through the mulberry paper to add an extra design feature. Other punched motifs could be used in the same way, such as a large heart.

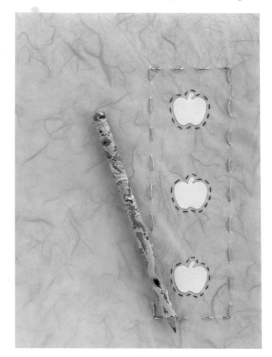

Ahoy There!

An ideal card for keen sailors or for any 'bon voyage' occasion, a suitable greeting could easily be added to personalize it. The waves of this card were embossed using a small section from a larger metal stencil (see pages 88–91). The boat and sails were cut from scraps of leftover paper, with cotton thread sewn in for the halyards. A similar design featuring a fleet of ships would make a lovely picture, which could be framed.

Ideal Home

This is a perfect card for those moving into a new home or as an encouragement to somebody in the process of renovating. Coordinating papers were used to make the miniature wallpaper sample books, and a border punch provides the base card with an additional decorative detail. An appropriate message could be added to the front of one of the sample books.

Collector's Item

This plain picture frame has been enlivened with a découpage design of colourful stamps, arranged so that they wrap around the edges of the frame. Once dried, the surface was given three coats of varnish. Instead of stamps, try a composition of images cut from a magazine, which could be uniformly square and used to create a mosaic-style effect.

Weave & Fold

WEAVING • LACÉ® • TEA BAG FOLDING
IRIS FOLDING • MIZUHIKI

Here, weaving is given a contemporary twist with the application of today's tools and papers, while the ceremonial art of mizuhiki is drawn into the 21st century by the allure of its luxurious paper cords. Tea bag folding has its roots in origami, but the availability of specialist papers has brought it within the reach of mainstream papercrafting. Lacé®, however, is a relatively modern craft, with unique templates and tools for cutting and tucking to create intricate designs. Weaving offers an ideal introduction to manipulating paper, but you can quickly produce some unexpected, dazzling effects by using colourful printed papers. For some, paper folding will become almost compulsive, especially when you can make such dynamic geometric patterns and decorations with the tea bag folding and iris folding techniques. Mix & Match showcases these crafts used in combination to make impactful and innovative items.

Clockwise from left: Glitzy Gift Tags, page 43; Chevron-Patterned Notepad Cover, pages 48–49; Rosette Hat Card, pages 52–53; Love Knot Card, page 59; Lacé® Daisy Card, pages 46–47; Blazing Sun Card, pages 56–57

Weaving

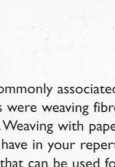

This highly traditional technique is most commonly associated with weaving threads to create fabric, and our ancestors were weaving fibres to create baskets even before they invented pottery. Weaving with paper is rather less well-known, but it is a useful technique to have in your repertoire as it can create lovely surfaces full of texture and interest that can be used for backgrounds, borders or just on their own.

Basic Tool Kit

METAL TEMPLATE
This template has slots cut into it through which you place a craft knife and make cuts in the paper underneath. Paper strips are then woven through the slots created. Several patterns to choose from are included on a single template.

TEMPLATE WEAVING TOOL
This is an optional tool that helps weave the paper strips through the slots created by the metal template. A paper strip is inserted into the tool and then the tool is used in the same way as a threaded needle to thread in and out of the slots.

Papers

Papers of 150gsm or less are suitable for paper weaving as they can be threaded in and out easily. Thicker papers will not thread easily and crease or buckle. Quilling papers are ideal for this craft as they come in ready-cut strips of different widths in a wide spectrum of colours. The papers in which you cut the slots should be of a similar weight – thick paper is too rigid and very fine paper, such as tissue paper, is too flimsy. Any paper design can be used for paper weaving, and it is a brilliant way of recycling paper such as giftwrap.

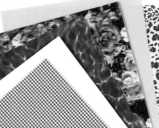

Basic Technique

Weaving is a technique that many of us know how to do but don't remember where or how we learnt it!

When choosing papers, select two or more colours that will work with each other when woven together. Once the basics have been grasped, you will then be able to experiment with different widths of paper and a variety of textures, which takes a simple technique to a new level.

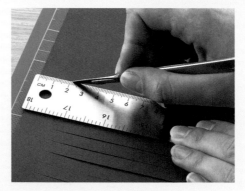

1 Take a sheet of paper in the colour of your choice. Starting 1cm (⅜in) from the top of the paper, cut vertical slits at evenly spaced intervals right to the bottom of the paper. This will create a fringed effect with the uncut top edge of the paper only holding the strips together.

2 Cut separate strips of the same width and length from a complementary coloured paper. Start by threading one strip horizontally over the first fringed length and then under the second fringed length. Continue to the end of the row, alternating over and under. Take another strip and weave it through the fringed lengths as before, but begin by threading under rather than over. When all the strips have been woven, it is a good idea to secure the ends with adhesive tape or glue.

Project Glitzy Gift Tags

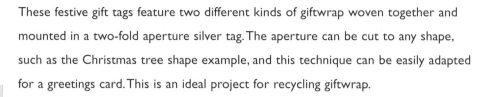

These festive gift tags feature two different kinds of giftwrap woven together and mounted in a two-fold aperture silver tag. The aperture can be cut to any shape, such as the Christmas tree shape example, and this technique can be easily adapted for a greetings card. This is an ideal project for recycling giftwrap.

You will need

pencil

★

metal ruler

★

two 6cm (2⅜in) squares of different giftwrap

★

craft knife

★

cutting mat

★

scissors

★

double-sided adhesive tape

★

two-fold silver gift tag 6.5cm (2½in) square with an aperture 3.5cm (1⅜in) square in the central panel

★

regular hole punch

★

narrow ribbon

 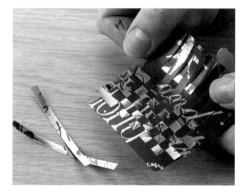

1 Using a pencil, mark every 5mm (³⁄₁₆in) across one giftwrap square top and bottom. Starting 1cm (⅜in) from the top edge and using a craft knife against a metal ruler, cut vertical lines at your pencil marks to make a fringe.

2 Cut the other piece of giftwrap into strips 5mm (³⁄₁₆in) wide. Weave one strip horizontally through the fringed giftwrap, threading over the first fringed length, then under, and repeat with the remaining strips, alternating the first weave.

3 Place lengths of double-sided adhesive tape around the aperture of the silver gift tag on the wrong side, then remove the backing from the tape. Hold the aperture right-side up over the woven square and lower into place. Press down firmly. Apply lengths of double-sided adhesive tape to the edges of the central panel of the tag on the wrong side, fold over the third panel and press down firmly, so that you have a single-fold tag. Punch a hole through the tag and thread ribbon through.

The strips of paper don't have to be of equal widths; in fact, the effect can be more interesting if different widths are used.

Lacé®

The term 'Lacé' comes from a French word meaning 'linked together'. The craft is so called because it involves cutting lines in paper using a metal template, scoring across the cuts, then folding these parts over and tucking them under each other so that they form a delicate pattern. You will need to buy specific metal templates for Lacé®, but once purchased, they can be used in a multitude of ways. Lacé® is the brand name for templates and tools produced by a company called Kars in the Netherlands. Because the products have become so popular with papercrafters, the brand name has been given to this technique.

Basic Tool Kit

LACÉ® METAL TEMPLATES

These are essential to Lacé®. Each template has a number of cutout lines that form a regular pattern. Different templates offer a different design, such as a rectangle or a circle, and the range is constantly expanding, but a single template can be used in a variety of ways – see the project on pages 46–47 and its variations.

CUTTING KNIFE

This has a stumpier blade than an ordinary craft knife, allowing it to be placed through the slots in the metal template with ease in order to cut the paper underneath.

SCORING AND FOLDING TOOL

A dual-purpose tool, this has a metal ball-shaped implement on one end for scoring paper and a plastic blade on the other end for folding.

LOW-TACK ADHESIVE TAPE

This tape is used to hold the metal template in place on the paper while cutting through the slots and can be peeled off without damaging the paper surface.

LACÉ® RULER (OPTIONAL)

Being smaller than an ordinary ruler, a Lacé® ruler is easier to handle for scoring.

CUTTING MAT

A cutting mat is essential to protect your work surface when cutting through the templates.

Papers

Duo-coloured card is available specifically for this craft. It comprises two different colours, one on each side of the card. When the cut shapes are folded over, they display the colour that is on the reverse side of the card. Duo card, at 250gsm, is on the borderline between a thick paper and a lightweight card. Two different-coloured sheets of thin paper can be glued together to create a similar material. Vellum is often used and is easier to cut through but does not cut as cleanly as duo card. Alternatively, a single-coloured piece of paper can be used with a contrasting colour placed underneath to show through the cutout sections.

Basic Technique

The following steps demonstrate the making of one Lacé® design out of the many available, but the principles involved form the basic technique. The cutting and scoring needs to be clean and precise, and a delicate touch is required for the folding and tucking stages.

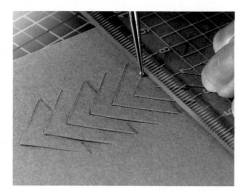

1 Place the duo card on the cutting mat. Position the Lacé® template on the paper and secure with low-tack adhesive tape. Place the cutting knife in the first slot on the template and cut at a 45-degree angle following the template.

2 As you reach the end of the slot, bring the knife up to a vertical angle. If you don't do this, you will not cut right to the very end of the slot. Because you are using duo card, you may have to press harder with the cutting knife than you usually would with paper – it may take some practice to get used to this.

3 Peel off the tape and remove the template. Position the ruler horizontally at the base of one inverted 'V' cut. Using the scoring end of the scoring and folding tool, score two lines from the cut base to the next inverted 'V' cut, leaving an unscored section in between. Move down the paper, leaving the next inverted 'V' cut unscored, and score the next cut as before. Continue scoring alternate cuts all the way down the design.

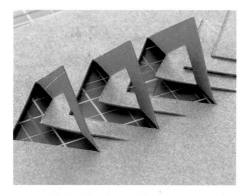

4 Lift up those sections that you have just scored. If you have not cut right the way through the paper or the cuts don't meet at the point, they will not lift up and you may need to cut again with the knife.

5 Carefully tuck the first section that you have lifted up under the unfolded section below. Repeat for the rest of the design.

SCORING AND FOLDING
Be patient when scoring the lines in Step 3. The point of scoring is to allow the cut section to fold over easily. This stops the paper from becoming misshapen and allows a crisp result. Do not score any part that is not going to be folded.
  The folding end of the scoring and folding tool can be used after Step 4 to make the folds more crisp.

Depending on the cuts and folds made, different looks can be achieved using the same stencil and duo card. See the Notepad Cover project on page 48.

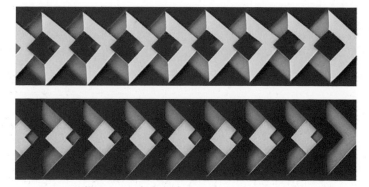

STORING LACE® TEMPLATES
Keep your Lacé® templates together, either in plastic sleeves or a separate storage drawer, as they are quite thin and easily slide under papers where they can stay hidden.

Project Lacé® Daisy Card

This card uses the same basic Lacé® technique but with curved lines, instead of straight ones, to produce a softer, rounded shape. Here, silver and blue duo card is used to create a striking design applicable to any occasion.

1 Place the duo card silver-side down on the cutting mat. Place the template on the duo card and fix in place with low-tack adhesive tape. Using a marker pen, mark a cross on the template where you start. Place the cutting knife in the outermost slot of the set of arcs closest to you and cut. Cut the two outermost and two innermost arcs, leaving the centre arc uncut.

You will need

silver and blue duo
card 11cm (4¼in) square
★
cutting mat
★
Lacé® template no 25
★
low-tack adhesive tape
★
marker pen
★
cutting knife
★
metal ruler
★
scoring and folding tool
★
metallic blue single-fold card
12cm (4¾in) square
★
double-sided adhesive tape

2 Keeping the template and card together, turn the work round to cut the next set of arcs in the same way. Continue until you are back at the pen cross and all the sections of the design are cut. If you get lost and don't know if you have cut a section, lift up both template and card to see what has been cut.

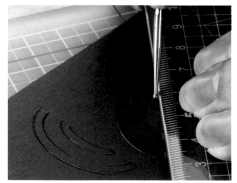

3 Remove the tape and template. Place a ruler across the base of the 4 cut lines of one set of arcs. Starting from the centre and using the scoring end of the scoring and folding tool, score between the two inner cut lines and the two outer cut lines. Repeat with the other sections of the design.

Cut around the very outer edge of the template to create a daisy-shaped card, which could be mounted onto a gift bag or box.

5 Use the folding end of the scoring and folding tool to press over the lifted-up sections to make a crisper fold. Move the card round as you do this.

4 Lift up the cut sections carefully using your fingers so that you can see the silver side of the duo card – if they have been cut and scored correctly, they should lift up easily.

When mounting the design, take care where you place the double-sided adhesive tape, or it will show through the cutout sections.

6 Tuck the outer silver section under the adjacent unfolded blue section. Continue in the same way all the way round the card. Mount the design onto the blue single-fold card using double-sided adhesive tape.

Further Technique

There are many different templates available that feature several design options – cutting different parts of the template, then folding the paper in varying directions, will give you a range of options. Experiment to see the effects you can achieve.

This sample shows how a single curved Lacé® template (left) can be used to create different designs by changing which slots in the template were cut. Any one of these ovals could be used for the Daisy Card design.

The templates shown offer at least two designs each. The octagonal side of the nearest template was used in Octagonal Art, page 61, and the slots were varied just as the sample above demonstrates. The other side to this template is a half-heart shape that could be used for a different project.

Project Chevron-Patterned Notepad Cover

This notepad cover will jazz up any desk and would make a memorable gift. The colours used could be tailored to suit the recipient's taste or their office decor.

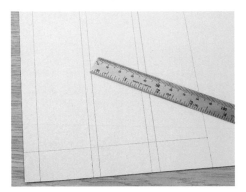

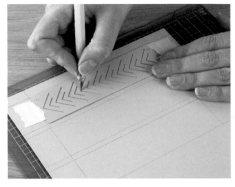

You will need

red and yellow duo card
27 x 18cm (10¾ x 7in)
★
pencil
★
metal ruler
★
cutting mat
★
Lacé© template no 2
★
low-tack adhesive tape
★
cutting knife
★
scoring and folding tool
★
double-sided adhesive tape
★
pink paper 18 x 13cm (7 x 5in)
★
PVA (white) glue
★
notepad 15 x 10.5cm (6 x 4¼in)

1 On the yellow side of the duo card, draw vertical lines at 1cm (⅜in), 4.5cm (1¾in), 5cm (2in), 8.5cm (3⅜in), 9cm (3½in) and 12.5cm (4⅞in) from the left-hand short edge. Draw a horizontal line 2.5cm (1in) from the top and bottom edge. You will now have three bordered strips.

2 Place the duo card on the cutting mat and position the template, with the 'V's of the design inverted, in the first measured strip. Secure with low-tack adhesive tape and, starting at the point of the slot, pull the cutting knife towards you in a single motion. You may then find it easier to turn the paper slightly to cut the other side of the slot, but make sure that the template does not move. Cut along all the slots. Move the template to the other outer strip and cut all the slots in the same way.

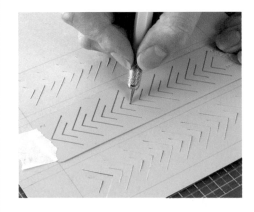

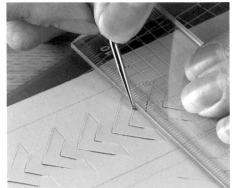

3 Remove the tape and template, then turn the duo card upside down. Position the template in the central strip, securing it with low-tack adhesive tape. Cut all the slots as before – they will be pointing in the opposite direction to those in the outer two strips. Carefully remove the tape and template.

4 Turn the duo card back to its original position. Score the cuts in the two outer rectangles. Position a ruler horizontally at the base of one cut and, using the scoring end of the scoring and folding tool, score two lines from the cut base to the next inverted 'V' cut, leaving an unscored section in between.

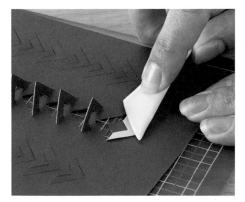 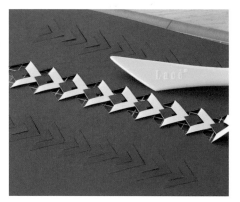 

5 Turn the duo card over to the red side and upside down and score the cuts in the central strip in the same way. Lift up each section and fold over with your fingers to reveal the yellow side of the paper. Using the folding end of the scoring and folding tool, press down along each of the folds in the central strip.

6 Take the first of the folded yellow sections and tuck this under the unfolded red section below. Continue working down the entire strip in the same way.

7 Turn the duo card over and back to its original position. Lift up the cut sections in the two outer strips, fold and tuck as before. Using double-sided adhesive tape, attach the piece of pink paper to the yellow side of the duo card – the pink will show through. Finish off by scoring two lines at 13cm (5in) and 14cm (5½in) from one edge for the spine of the notebook cover. Glue the notepad to the inside of the cover.

This project could be adapted to make a bookmark by cutting only one of the chevron panels and mounting it onto a length of card with a tassel at one end.

Tea Bag Folding

Tea bag folding intrigues many people by its name alone. And no, it doesn't use tea bags, which disappoints everyone. The term comes from the paper bags that traditionally encased many fruit teas. Tiny Van Der Plas and Janet Wilson developed a technique of folding squares of paper cut from these small paper bags. Several of these folded squares are then linked together to form a rosette shape. Sometimes referred to as kaleidoscope folding, tea bag folding is actually a form of origami, and although it looks complicated to a beginner, it is not difficult in practice. It has many applications, such as decorating cards or embellishing pages in scrapbooking.

Basic Tool Kit

SCISSORS
A good-quality, sharp pair of scissors is required, the size depending on the scale of the individual project.

METAL RULER
The paper has to be accurately measured, if not using ready-printed paper squares (see Papers below), and precisely cut to ensure a successful result.

PVA (WHITE) GLUE AND COCKTAIL STICK
Use PVA (white) glue, applied with a cocktail stick, for tea bag folding – it is easy to use and quick-drying.

Papers

Some people still use the traditional paper bags that fruit teas come in for this craft, but these are not readily available to everyone. Instead, most papercrafters use specialist sheets of paper that are printed with designs in squares ready to cut out. However, any medium-weight paper with a pattern that folds neatly can be used, although not all patterns work well when folded. One patterned square of paper can be folded in different ways and so the design of the end result will vary even when a square of the same paper design is used. There are also specific tea bag papers available for those who don't like folding. They are printed with rosette shapes ready to cut out and arrange.

Basic Technique

Squares of equal size are cut from paper. A series of folds are then made to each square in the same way, origami-style, to produce a folded shape. These folded shapes are then slotted and glued together to form a decorative motif, in this case a rosette. There are an infinite number of ways in which a paper square can be folded, but only one is shown here.

ESSENTIALS OF TEA BAG FOLDING

Before you begin, read through these important rules for perfect tea bag folding, and bear them in mind as you practise.

- The paper squares must be exactly the same size to begin with, otherwise any small discrepancy will become apparent in the end result.

- All folds must be crisp and precise – any uneven or bumpy folds will show up.

- If you are a beginner, start with large squares, then decrease the size of the squares as you grow in confidence.

- Once folded, the squares must be carefully assembled and glued together, otherwise the resulting rosette shape will be uneven.

1 With right sides facing, fold a square of paper in half.

2 Open out and, with wrong sides facing (i.e. with the pattern on the outside), fold in half diagonally.

3 Open out and, again with wrong sides facing, fold in half along the other diagonal.

4 You will find that the square starts to take shape, so place your two forefingers into the first horizontal fold you made and push them together. The paper folds inwards and a triangle is created.

Project Rosette Hat Card

Tea bag folding is used here to make an eye-catching and unique greetings card, featuring a rosette attached to a hat-shaped card as part of a decorative hat band. This highly attractive embellishment could be used to decorate many other items, such as a gift box or bag.

You will need

sheet of harvest quilt
tea bag folding paper
★
scissors
★
cocktail stick
★
PVA (white) glue
★
pencil
★
scrap card
★
purple card
21 x 30cm (8¼ x 12in)
★
purple paper
17 x 1cm (6¾ x ⅜in)
★
green paper
17cm x 3mm (6¾ x ⅛in)

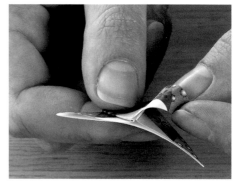

1 Cut eight 5cm (2in) squares from the harvest quilt paper. Follow the steps in the Basic Technique section on page 51 to fold each square into a triangle. You will see that each triangle has four corners. Take one corner of one triangle and fold it under, towards the point of the triangle.

2 Take the other corner of the same side and fold it under in the same way.

3 You should now have a triangular shape but with a folded square on the front. Fold the other seven squares in the same way.

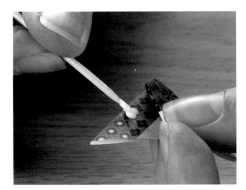

4 Hold one triangular piece and, using a cocktail stick, apply a dab of glue under one side of the folded square.

5 Take another triangular piece and slot this into the glued one. The folded squares should now be glued together.

6 Keep gluing and slotting the triangular pieces together until a circle begins to take shape.

If this is your first attempt at a tea bag folding project, assemble the complete rosette before gluing the pieces together to check whether any have not been properly folded.

7 The eight pieces will fit neatly together to form a rosette. Make your own card template from the hat template on page 129 (see Step 1, page 16). Fold the purple card in half widthways. Position the template on the folded card, making sure that the top of the hat aligns with the fold of the card, draw around the template and cut out. Using glue applied with a cocktail stick, attach the purple paper strip to the card first, then stick the green paper strip along the middle of the purple strip. Finally, attach the finished rosette to the card.

Tea bag folding doesn't have to create a rosette shape. Four of these folded pieces each glued to a corner of a greetings card would complement another, central design.

Iris Folding

In this technique, patterned strips of paper are overlapped from the outer edge inwards until they eventually meet, forming a spiral. This spiral resembles the iris of an eye or a camera and this is how the technique got its name. The work is done on the reverse of the image and only when completed do you turn it over to view your creation. Iris folding originated in the Netherlands, where the colourful insides of envelopes were recycled for this papercraft. The size and shape of the aperture in the card used is an important feature.

Basic Tool Kit

FOLDING TEMPLATES
Folding templates are needed, such as the example shown here and on page 128. You can design your own template once you have gained experience and confidence in the technique of iris folding.

SMALL SCISSORS
A good-quality, small, fine-pointed pair of scissors is needed for trimming the paper strips used in iris folding.

CLEAR ADHESIVE TAPE
This is used for attaching the strips of paper to card.

Papers

While this craft began by utilizing the patterns from the inside of envelopes, unfortunately not all countries have such good envelope manufacturers to provide us with this decorative material. Specific papers for iris folding are available, but any patterned, lightweight papers can be used. It is essential to use lightweight paper or the many layers of folded papers become too bulky. Holographic card is frequently used in iris folding, placed behind the aperture in the centre of the folded shape.

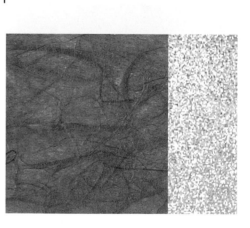

Basic Technique

Iris folding has many variations, but once the basic overlapping technique is understood, it is a good foundation from which to develop. You need to choose papers that complement each other. Here, three colours are used to demonstrate the basic triangle shape. If using another aperture shape, such as a square or circle, you may wish to use four or five different papers for the folded strips of paper, but there is no set rule as to how many sets of coloured papers you can use.

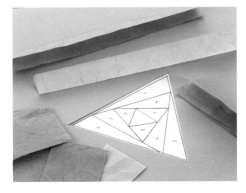

1 Photocopy the iris folding template on page 128 and cut out. Place underneath a piece of card with a triangular aperture cut to the same shape and size as the template. Cut three strips of paper from each of three colours, in this case blue, dark green and light green, and fold in half lengthways.

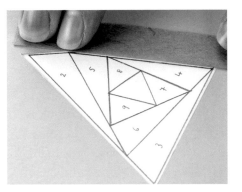

2 Place a dark green strip over line 1, with the fold facing inwards. Secure to the card with small pieces of clear adhesive tape.

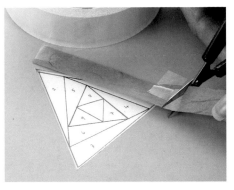

3 Trim the excess paper with scissors, taking care that the remaining paper overlaps the edge of the aperture.

4 Place a strip of blue paper over line 2, overlapping the first strip. Secure with tape and trim. Place a strip of light green paper over line 3, again overlapping the other strips. Secure and trim.

5 Continue in this way, positioning the coloured strips in the same colour order following the numbers on the template until all nine lengths of paper are taped in place. Tape a small piece of holographic paper over the hole left in the centre.

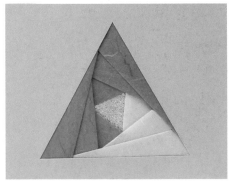

6 Now turn the card over and view the results from the front.

CONSISTENT POSITIONING

The folds of the strips of paper must always be positioned facing inwards, otherwise the the crisp, clean effect will be spoilt.

Project Blazing Sun Card

This dynamic sun design positively emanates warmth and happiness – an ideal card to send to anyone in need of cheer, or to brighten up the cold winter months.

You will need

30 strips of paper
10 x 2cm (4 x ¾in),
5 in each of 3 shades of orange and
5 in each of 3 shades of yellow

★

small scissors

★

two-fold red card 12.5cm (4⅞in) square with a round aperture 9cm (3½in) in diameter

★

clear adhesive tape

★

holographic card
7 x 9cm (2¾ x 3½in)

★

double-sided adhesive tape

★

yellow card 10cm (4in) square

★

glue stick

You may want to use low-tack adhesive tape to hold the card over the template and keep it firmly in place.

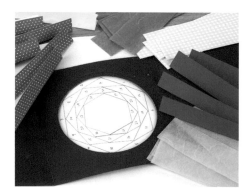

1 Fold all the strips in half lengthways and group according to their six colours. Photocopy the template on page 128 and cut out. Place the template on your work surface, then place the two-fold card, opened out and right-side down, over the template so that you can see the template through the circular aperture of the card.

2 Place one strip of yellow paper, folded edge inwards, over line 1. Trim the ends and tape in place. Continue positioning the paper strips using a different colour each time and following the numbered sequence as marked on the template.

3 Keep working round the circle with the strips of paper, applying the strips in the same colour order with the folded edge inwards and following the numbered sequence. It will start to look untidy but don't worry as this is the unseen side!

4 As you get closer to the centre, the strips will get smaller, so you will need to trim off more.

5 When the last strip has been used, tape the holographic card, glossy-side down, over the remaining hole in the centre.

6 Attach lengths of double-sided adhesive tape to all four edges of the central panel of the card on the inside. Remove the tape backing, fold the third section of the card over and press down firmly to make a single-fold card. Cut 12 triangles from the yellow card 2cm (¾in) high x 2cm (¾in) wide. Glue these to the front of the card around the aperture.

Add an appropriate greeting of your choice to a piece of paper and attach it to the holographic paper in the centre of the card.

Mizuhiki

Mizuhiki is the name given to the craft of tying Japanese ceremonial paper cord. It originated in China in the 7th century, when the Chinese Emperor sent a gift to the Japanese Emperor tied with ornate paper cord. The Japanese Emperor was so enchanted with these paper cords that he ordered them to be made, after which mizuhiki took off in Japan. Traditionally, the art of mizuhiki is reserved for creating ceremonial knots to be worn on clothing. However, the beauty of these shining cords has now proved tempting to many papercrafters.

Basic Tool Kit

SCISSORS
Good-quality, sharp scissors are needed for cutting mizuhiki cords. Keep to hand a small pair for trimming cord, and a larger pair (see step 2 below) for cutting several lengths of cord at once.

NARROW DOUBLE-SIDED ADHESIVE TAPE
This adhesive tape is used for attaching the mizuhiki cords to card.

Mizuhiki cords bend easily but will not stand too much handling before they become misshapen. Store carefully so that they don't get crushed by heavy weights.

These cords came in two separate packs of greens and pinks, but don't be afraid to mix and match colours between the packs.

Papers

The paper cords used in mizuhiki are now available across the world and come in many lovely bright colours, which are a delight to a crafter's eyes. They are relatively thin, bend easily and are cut with ordinary scissors. The inner cord is wrapped with metallic paper and, with excessive bending, this layer will start to come loose. The paper cords generally come in long lengths, which can easily be cut to size.

Basic Technique

Many different traditional knots can be tied with mizuhiki cords but the basic techniques remain the same. Mizuhiki knots are generally applied to cards, but they could be used as decorations on gift packaging or even made into jewellery.

For inspiration on different knots to create using mizuhiki cords, look for examples of nautical rope knots in specialist reference books.

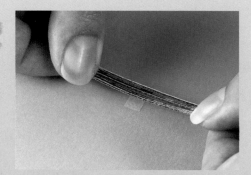

1 Place double-sided adhesive tape on your card where the cords will go and remove the backing – the tape is placed at right-angles to the cords, but an extra line of tape can be added along the length of the cords. Take five lengths of mizuhiki cord and attach them to the tape. With a straight line, you can place all the lengths down together, but if you are creating a knot, position one at a time.

2 Mizuhiki cords can have a life of their own and will spring off a surface if not stuck down properly on the tape, so make sure they are firmly in place. Using scissors, trim the ends of the cords.

Love Knot Card

This simple yet sumptuous card really shows off the fabulous qualities of mizuhiki cords. Mizuhiki is said to connect the hearts of the giver and receiver. With this in mind, the symbolic entwined knot design featured here would be perfect to mark a special wedding anniversary.

You will need

narrow double-sided adhesive tape
★
lime single-fold card
12cm (4¾in) square
★
6 dark green mizuhiki cords
20cm (8in) long
★
4 gold and green mizuhiki cords
20cm (8in) long
★
4 lime green mizuhiki cords
20cm (8in) long
★
scissors
★
2 dark pink, 4 gold and pink and
4 shiny pink mizuhiki cords
11cm (4¼in) long

This card could be made with three or five lengths of mizuhiki cord in each loop — any number can be used as long as it's an odd number.

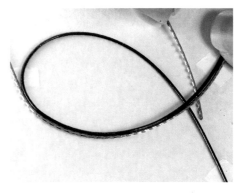

1 Attach three 5mm (³⁄₁₆in) lengths of double-sided adhesive tape to the front of the card where the first loop will lie and remove the backing. Make a simple loop with one length of dark green mizuhiki cord. Place this onto the tape with the ends of the cord hanging off the card.

2 Weave a length of gold and green mizuhiki cord around and under the first loop, and stick this in place onto the tape.

3 Continue weaving either side of the first dark green loop so that there are three cords on each side — gold and green, lime green, then dark green. Trim the ends with scissors. Make another loop in exactly the same way so that it is linked with the first loop. Attach five pink mizuhiki cords to the top and bottom of the card in the same way to make a border.

Mix & Match

Creative Pathways

Lacé® and tea bag folding were combined in this novelty card design. Recycled maps were folded using the basic folding sequence on page 45. These were mounted onto another section of a map that had been cut and folded with a Lacé® template. This was mounted into the aperture of a card covered with lime green handmade paper. You could use nautical maps for a sailing enthusiast or sheet music for a music lover.

Messages from the Heart

Tiny envelopes were made from patterned vellum, filled with script paper and tied with embroidery thread. These were then glued to a single-fold orange card. A wide strip of the patterned vellum was attached to the centre of the card. Strips of script paper and vellum were woven together and mounted in a heart-shaped aperture, which was in turn mounted onto the patterned vellum with adhesive foam pads. The colours of the card could be chosen to coordinate with the colour scheme of a wedding, or mount just one envelope on a card, to enclose a secret message to your valentine.

Fashion Statement

The tea bag folding technique featured in the project on pages 52–53 was used to create an elegant rosette from pink checked paper. It was then mounted onto a purple handbag-shaped card. Mizuhiki cord was twisted to form the handle and attached to the card. The shape of the handbag can be changed to keep up with the latest fashion.

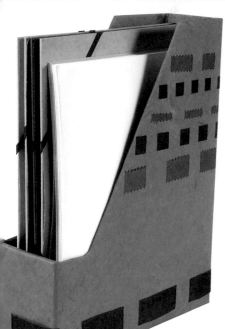

Sartorial Stationery

A single sheet of pink plaid paper was collaged to create this shirt card (see pages 26–27), with a tie shape cut out of the collage and made into a separate tag. Strips of folded paper in coordinating colours were attached to the reverse side of the collage, where the tie had been cut out, in one direction in a variation on the iris folding technique. The colours used can be tailored to the recipient. A gift tag is made using the same tie shape.

File Style

A sheet of blue handmade paper was woven with strips of pink and navy blue handmade paper of varying widths. This was then used to cover a box file, the paper being glued to the file using a glue stick. Choose different colour combinations to match the recipient's home office decor.

Octagonal Art

Using Lacé® template no 41, octagonal shapes were cut from a strip of silver and blue duo card, which was then attached to a single-fold card. The corners were cut off the single-fold card to make it a matching octagonal shape and strips of silver and blue paper were added to complete the design. Any colour of duo card, combined with a third complementary colour for the base card, could be used to create variations on the same design.

Precious Metal

A round box was covered with blue handmade paper. A loop of 1cm (⅜in) wide metallic quilling paper was then threaded through the centre of a tea bag rosette. This was then glued to the lid of the box and the rim of the lid trimmed with the same metallic paper as the loop.

Curl & Coil

In this absorbing papercraft, the art of coiling narrow strips of paper into delicate shapes, then arranging these shapes together results in designs that can be as simple or as complex as you wish. In fact, the creative possibilities of quilling are limitless! In the pages that follow, you will see how this historic craft has been developed and adapted to create bold, contemporary effects, shaking off its familiar traditional image.

But however ambitious you wish to be in your quilling work, the craft involves building on just one basic technique, from which you can produce a range of intricate patterns and pictures, all with an intriguing three-dimensional element. In this chapter, you will also discover an additional, innovative refinement of the technique — fringing — and the Mix & Match section reveals how you can use the many varied forms of quilling to great effect in conjunction with other techniques.

Clockwise from left: Patter of Tiny Feet, page 72; Three Little Fishes Card, page 67; Hedgehog Harvest Frame, pages 70–71; Chorus Line, page 111; Prettily Packaged, page 72; Frilly Flower Card, page 69

Quilling

Paper quilling, or paper filigree, is the craft of coiling thin strips of paper. These coils are glued, then pinched into different shapes. Quilling took off in Europe during the 18th century, when ladies coiled strips of paper around the quills of feathers. Wooden boxes, fire screens and other objects would be elaborately decorated with these paper coils.

Nowadays, quilling has progressed with the development of new techniques and the availability of a wide range of interesting papers, making it a highly popular craft. The appeal of this papercraft is that with just a simple tool, paper strips and glue, many different shapes can be created and combined to produce wonderfully ornate designs and embellishments.

Basic Tool Kit

FRINGING TOOL

This clever gadget cuts the quilling papers at regular intervals, leaving a fringed strip of paper, which is then coiled to create a frilled effect. Fringing tools come in two types: those that cut at a 90-degree angle to the edge of the paper, which is shown here, and those that cut at a 45-degree angle. Most of these tools are made for 1cm (⅜in) wide strips of paper. Although a relatively costly item, this tool is highly recommended.

QUILLING TOOL

This has a two-pronged metal head mounted on a wooden handle. A paper strip is threaded through the prongs, then coiled by turning the wooden handle.

RIBBLER

This paper ribbler, or crimper, turns flat paper into contoured, wavy paper. Ribblers come in a variety of sizes to accommodate paper of varying widths, up to a maximum of 8cm (3¼in). Ribbled paper is great for adding texture and dimension to backgrounds for card designs. Ribbled paper strips can also be made into very loose coils, with or without the aid of a quilling tool, to create leaves and other decorative details.

Papers

There is a huge variety of quilling papers available and here is a just a sample. Quilling papers are available for purchase in standard widths: 3mm (⅛in), 5mm (³⁄₁₆in), 1cm (⅜in) and 1.5cm (⅝in). The 3mm (⅛in) wide papers are most commonly used and are ideal for the beginner. Specialist retailers will cut papers to any width you require. You can always cut your own paper strips – you don't have to rely on quilling suppliers for your papers.

Quilling papers need to be stored properly, otherwise they easily become tangled and damaged – see page 7 for further advice.

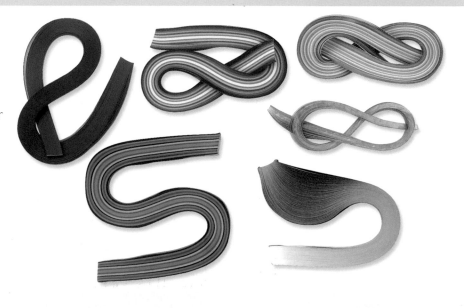

Basic Technique Coiling

To start quilling, a quilling tool is recommended, but it is possible to make coils just by using your fingers. However, throughout this chapter it is assumed that a quilling tool will be used, since this is the easiest and most effective method.

CLOSED COILS

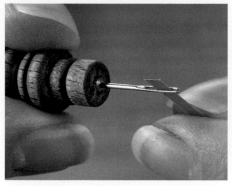

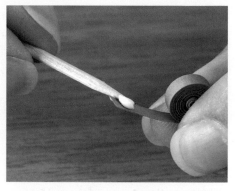

1 Holding the quilling tool in one hand, with the other hand, slot one end of a 20cm (8in) length of 3mm (⅛in) wide paper through the metal prongs. Only feed 5mm (³⁄₁₆in) through the prongs to start with as this is just enough to hold the paper when turning the tool.

2 Rotate the quilling tool, keeping the paper taut with the other hand. As you turn the quilling tool, the paper is wound round the tool, forming a tight circle of paper, but the tension must be constantly maintained with the other hand.

3 Remove the quilling tool from the centre of the tight coil. Using a cocktail stick, apply a dab of PVA (white) glue to the end of the paper strip. Press this glued end to the coil to prevent it from unwinding. This is a tight closed coil because the paper strip has not been allowed to unwind at all before the end was glued in place.

LOOSE CLOSED COILS

Experiment by allowing the coil to unwind a little before gluing the end in place, to make a loose closed coil.

BASIC CLOSED COIL SHAPES
This is a selection of coils made from 20cm (8in) lengths of 3mm (⅛in) wide paper.
At the top is a tight coil, while the other coils were made by letting the coil unwind by different amounts before gluing, to create different sizes.

ADDING TEXTURE – RIBBLING
Strips of paper are fed between the two cogs of a paper ribbler, which have a pattern on them – wavy, in this case. By turning the handle, the cogs rotate and the paper strip is drawn through and pressed into shape (see right).

Further Techniques Creating Shapes

The basic technique shown on page 65 can be built upon to create shapes from the closed coils. Alternatively, not gluing the coils at all, then allowing them to unwind, gives an altogether different look.

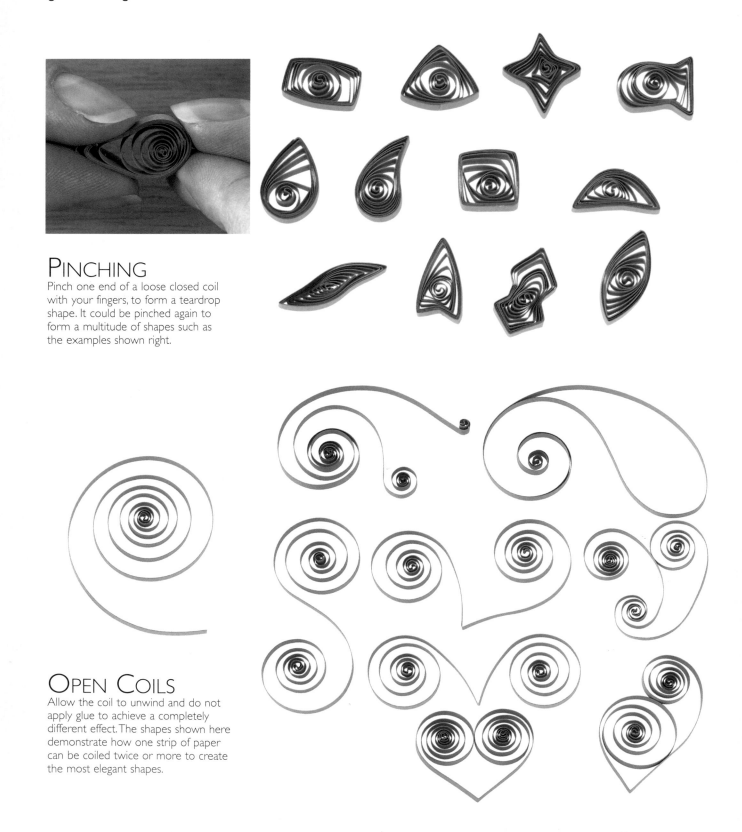

PINCHING

Pinch one end of a loose closed coil with your fingers, to form a teardrop shape. It could be pinched again to form a multitude of shapes such as the examples shown right.

OPEN COILS

Allow the coil to unwind and do not apply glue to achieve a completely different effect. The shapes shown here demonstrate how one strip of paper can be coiled twice or more to create the most elegant shapes.

Project Three Little Fishes Card

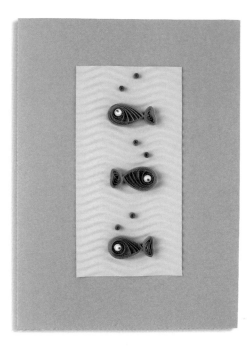

This contemporary, fun fish design will have wide appeal to people of any age group. It is also an ideal project for a beginner in quilling.

You will need

cocktail stick
★
PVA (white) glue
★
ribbler
★
blue paper
10.5 x 5cm (4¼ x 2in), ribbled
★
single-fold light blue card
15 x 10.5cm (6 x 4¼in)
★
orange 3mm (⅛in)
wide quilling paper strips
★
small scissors
★
quilling tool
★
dark blue 1.5mm (¹⁄₁₆in) wide
quilling paper strips
★
three wiggly eyes
★
superglue

1 Using a cocktail stick, glue the piece of ribbled paper to the front of the single-fold blue card. Using a quilling tool, make a loose closed coil with a 30cm (12in) length of orange paper strip. When the glue has dried, pinch one end to a point, making a teardrop shape. Try to pinch the point where the end of the paper was glued so that the join is on the apex of the pinched point.

2 Make a fairly tight closed coil using a 15cm (6in) length of orange paper strip and pinch this into a 'U' shape using your fingernails. Glue the two pieces together to form a fish shape. Make two more fish in this way. Glue all three fish, one below the other, onto the ribbled paper, each swimming in alternate directions.

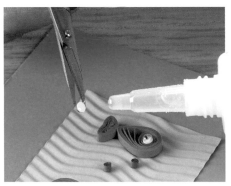

3 Make a tight closed coil from one 4cm (1½in) length of dark blue paper strip. Make five more tight coils for the fish bubbles. Attach two of the bubbles above each fish with glue.

4 Using one hand, pick up a wiggly eye between the points of a small pair of scissors and, with the other hand, dab a dot of superglue onto the back of the wiggly eye (this will prevent you from getting superglue on your fingers; superglue is recommended, otherwise the eyes tend to fall off). Position the eye on the head of one fish. Repeat with the remaining eyes.

If you are short of time, make one fish and mount onto a smaller square of paper on a single-fold card.

Further Technique **Fringing**

A strip of paper can be fringed using a pair of scissors, but a fringing tool is a much quicker method.

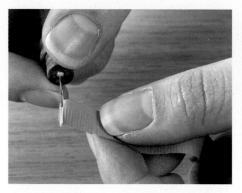

1 Place a 1cm (⅜in) wide strip of paper in the tool. Move the handle up and down – the paper is sliced widthways but not all the way across, leaving a narrow margin to keep the strips of paper in one piece. At the same time, the paper strip is pulled along so that it is automatically fed through the slicer.

2 Place one end of a fringed strip into the quilling tool, making sure that the edge that has been fringed is outermost. It is the narrow margin that is used for coiling. Rotate the quilling tool with one hand, maintaining the tension on the paper with the other hand. Keep turning the quilling tool in the same direction and the paper will form a coil.

3 When the fringed strip has been coiled, carefully remove the quilling tool. Using a cocktail stick, apply a dab of PVA (white) glue to the narrow margin. Press onto the rest of the coil and leave to dry.

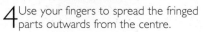

4 Use your fingers to spread the fringed parts outwards from the centre.

FRINGING TOOL
Some fringing tools have holes that allow them to be mounted onto a sturdy block of wood for easier use.

Project Frilly Flower Card

This spray of fringed and coiled flowers makes a highly attractive and innovative three-dimensional card design. Any number of flowers in a single colour, or a mixture, could be used to make a bouquet.

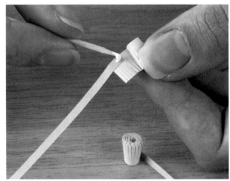

1 Fringe five 15cm (6in) lengths of the cream paper strips. Using a cocktail stick, glue a 4cm (1½in) length of yellow paper strip to the margin at one end of a fringed cream strip. Glue a 12cm (4¾in) length of light green paper strip to the margin on the other end of the fringed cream strip. Repeat this for all five lengths and leave the glue to dry. Place the yellow paper strip in the quilling tool and coil tightly until you reach the green strip.

2 Carefully remove the quilling tool. Using a cocktail stick, apply a dab of glue to the beginning of the green strip. Press this onto the rest of the coiled paper. When the glue has dried, open out the cream fringed part to reveal the yellow centre of the flower. Repeat with the remaining paper strips.

You will need

cream 1cm (⅜in) wide quilling
paper strips
★
scissors
★
fringing tool
★
cocktail stick
★
PVA (white) glue
★
yellow and light green 3mm (⅛in)
wide quilling paper strips
★
quilling tool
★
two-fold lilac card
18 x 12.5cm (7 x 4⅞in)
with oval aperture
★
purple card
17 x 12cm (6¾ x 4¾in)
mounted behind the aperture

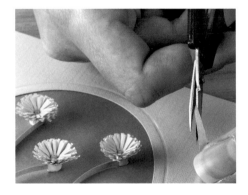

3 Apply a generous dab of glue to the underside of each coiled flower and attach them to the purple card in the centre of the aperture. Don't worry that the stems of the flowers are too long to fit within the aperture as these will be trimmed later.

4 Cut three lengths of light green paper strip 6cm (2⅜in), 8cm (3¼in) and 12cm (4¾in) long. Using scissors, trim one end of each of the lengths to a point. Run a fingernail along the lengths to slightly stretch and curl them. Glue to the flower stems to make leaves. Trim all the ends so that they fit neatly within the oval aperture.

When posting a quilled card, place two layers of bubble wrap in the envelope to protect it from being crushed.

Project Hedgehog Harvest Frame

This picture frame has been embellished with an endearing harvest theme, featuring appealing quilled hedgehogs munching on sprigs of luscious blackberries.

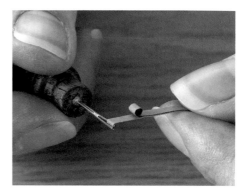

You will need

dark purple, red, brown, light green and dark green 3mm (⅛in) wide quilling paper strips

★

scissors

★

quilling tool

★

cocktail stick

★

PVA (white) glue

★

brown 1cm (⅜in) wide quilling paper strips

★

fringing tool

★

small scissors

★

three wiggly eyes

★

superglue

★

shadow box 28 x 23cm (11 x 9in) and 4.5cm (1¾in) deep with a cream picture mount inside

1 Cut the dark purple paper strips into about 70 lengths of between 2cm (¾in) and 5cm (2in) – the lengths need to vary in order to make coils of different sizes. Using a quilling tool, make a closed coil with each strip. Cut three lengths of the red paper strip varying between 2cm (¾in) and 5cm (2in) and make into closed coils. To make the blackberries, glue six or seven purple closed coils together, leaving a small gap for the stalk to be inserted later. Make 11 blackberries. One blackberry should have the three red closed coils so that it looks unripe.

2 Fold an 8cm (3¼in) length of 3mm (⅛in) wide brown paper strip in half. From the central fold, glue the paper up to 1cm (⅜in) from the ends, then fold these over so that they become double thickness but the two ends are still free. Use the quilling tool to coil each loose end away from each other in open coils. This then becomes the stalk of the blackberry.

3 Glue the coiled end of the stalk in place and insert into the small gap left between the blackberry coils. Make and attach stalks to the remaining blackberries. Take one stalk and trim the end, leaving only the coils attached to the blackberry. This is the black-berry that the hedgehogs will be eating as if it has fallen from the bush.

4 Fringe three 35cm (13¾in) lengths of 1cm (⅜in) wide brown paper strip and make three tight coils. Put these to one side. Make a 25cm (9⅞in) length of 3mm (⅛in) wide brown paper strip into a loose closed coil. Using your fingers, pinch it into a triangular shape. Make two more in the same way.

Spray varnish can be used to protect your quilled designs from dust and damp.

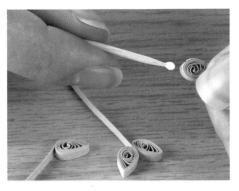

5 Glue a pinched triangular shape to a fringed coil to form a hedgehog. Using one hand, pick up a wiggly eye between the points of a small pair of scissors. With the other hand, apply a dab of superglue to the back of the wiggly eye. Position the eye on the pinched triangle.

6 Cut 33 lengths of light green paper strips between 12cm (4¾in) and 15cm (6in). Make each length into a closed coil, then pinch each into a teardrop shape.

7 Attach the round end of one light green coil to the end of a 10cm (4in) length of light green paper strip. Add another two light green coils to make a leaf. Repeat with the remaining light green coils so that you have 11 leaves.

8 Assemble the blackberries, hedgehogs and leaves on the cream picture mount using the finished photo as a guide. When you are happy with the composition, glue the leaf stalks to the blackberry stalks. When these are dry, glue all the items to the picture mount. Trim the ends of the stalks so that they fit neatly on the picture mount.

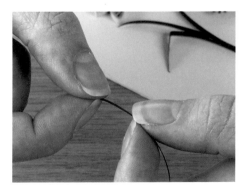

9 Cut seven lengths of dark green paper strip between 5cm (2in) and 8cm (3¼in) long. Cut one end of each length into a point. Holding the end, firmly drag your fingernail along the length to make the paper curl. Repeat for the remaining dark green lengths. Glue three together, attach to the mount, then trim the ends. Repeat with the other four lengths. Insert the completed picture mount into the shadow box.

Mix & Match

Floral Tribute

The three flowers were made using the fringing and coiling technique, with yellow centres and green stalks. A square of cream card was sewn to the back of a sheet of patterned vellum using a sewing machine. Two squares of the vellum paper were attached to the back of this in each corner to give it a deeper colour. The three flower stems were then glued to the card, framed within the central square. Instead of using patterned vellum, text could be printed onto coloured paper using a home computer and printer, personalized for a wedding or other special occasion.

Prettily Packaged

A small gift bag was made from orange giftwrap using the technique on page 17. Three fringed and coiled orange flowers were attached to the bag with green paper strips for leaves, curled with a fingernail. To create the butterfly wings, the end of a dark purple paper strip was glued to the end of a light purple strip, then a loose coil was made by starting to coil from the light purple end. It was then pinched into a teardrop shape and glued to the black body of the butterfly. A ribbon handle attached to the bag adds the finishing touch.

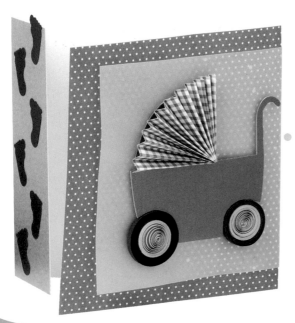

Patter of Tiny Feet

The pram wheels were made from four 40cm (15¾in) lengths of quilling paper, two dark purple and two light purple, glued end to end and coiled as one. Purple checked paper, folded concertina-style, was gathered together and glued on one side to form the pram hood. The body of the pram was cut from purple card and mounted with adhesive foam pads. Punched foot shapes were used to decorate the left-hand panel of the card (see page 22). If you want to follow tradition, choose blues and blue checked paper for a boy or pinks and pink checked paper for a girl.

Hit the Right Note

Tea bag folding and quilling were combined for this card. Old music sheets were cut into squares and folded using the tea bag folding method on pages 51–53. The resulting rosette was then glued in the square aperture of a two-fold cream card. For the musical notes, tight coils were made from black 3mm (⅛in) wide quilling paper, with a short length left unquilled. A strip of sheet music completes the design. If you are musical, you could use the quilled notes to make a proper tune – use a long, landscape-shaped card in this case.

Got Your Number!

To form the numeral 10, mizuhiki cord was attached to yellow paper (see pages 58–59), then sewn in place with cotton. The edge of the paper was trimmed with fancy-edged scissors and glued to spotted green paper. Quilled teardrop shapes were glued together to form flowers and attached to the corners of the yellow paper. The spiral shapes were punched (see page 22) then glued on at random. Any number, to suit the recipient or occasion, can be featured on the card.

A Gift of Love

Five scrolled heart shapes were stamped and then embossed with silver powder (see pages 104–105) onto a ready-made gift bag. The other four heart shapes were made from red 3mm (⅛in) wide quilling paper using the open coil technique and glued to the bag. The matching tag was made by embossing a square of silver paper with a heart, then trimming it with fancy-edged scissors.

Relief

PARCHMENT CRAFT • PRICKING • EMBOSSING

With each of these relief papercrafts,
a plain sheet of paper can be magically
transformed without the aid of scissors.
In parchment craft, a delicate, almost
ethereal image emerges from the surface, as
a result of the finely controlled application
of a few simple tools, while pricking relies on
the subtle interplay of light and shadow
cast by pierced holes. Embossing has
similar attributes, but ready-made stencils
give you the opportunity to create complex
patterns with professional results.
These traditional papercrafts are given
a modern makeover in this chapter with a
range of imaginative projects. Beginners
will be encouraged by the sheer simplicity of
pricking and yet delighted with the
sophisticated results, whereas parchment
craft has the capacity to push any
practised papercrafter's abilities to the full.
The Mix & Match section will inspire
you further to think in new, innovative
ways about these tried and trusted crafts.

*Clockwise from left: Classical Wedding
Stationery, pages 90–91; Floral Garland
Card, pages 84–85; Butterfly Card,
pages 78–79; Teddy Picture, pages
82–83; Fern Panels, page 87; Classical
Wedding Stationery, pages 90–91*

Parchment Craft

A long, rich heritage and the versatility of its effects has ensured the continuing – and growing – popularity of parchment craft.

The craft uses specialist parchment papers, which are translucent papers that change colour and become stretched when pressure is applied with tools. This technique is known as embossing. The essence of parchment craft is in varying the amount of embossing to the paper to control the shade and tone of colour produced in the design.

Traditionally, parchment craft designs were all white on a translucent paper, and the pure, simple beauty of this approach keeps it a firm favourite with many crafters today. But as the craft has increased in popularity over recent years, additional products such as pre-printed parchment vellums are now available, and more people are experimenting and achieving impressive effects by embellishing with colour. The designs can be further enhanced by pricking and cutting the parchment paper.

Basic Tool Kit

FOAM PAD An important part of the tool kit, this allows the paper to 'give' when embossing. Pads specially designed for parchment craft can be purchased, but a piece of dark-coloured craft foam is ideal.

MAPPING PEN or pen with a nib. This can be used, with white ink, as an alternative to white pencil for tracing designs. Specially designed mapping pens for parchment craft have a fine nib for accurate outlining, but any pen with a nib that can be dipped into a bottle of ink to fill up the reservoir can be used.

FINE BALL EMBOSSING TOOL This has a very fine ball and is useful for embossing detail in a design.

LARGE/MEDIUM BALL EMBOSSING TOOL The size of metal ball attached to the tool for embossing varies. Here, large and medium balls are on either end of the same tool, but these tools can also be purchased separately.

WHITE INK This is a specialist ink for use in parchment craft. It is usually water resistant once dried, but refer to individual manufacturer's instructions. Shake or stir the bottle before use as the sediment settles at the bottom of the container. Coloured or metallic inks can also be used.

WHITE PENCIL For tracing designs, you will need a standard white colouring pencil; do not use a watercolour pencil.

Papers

PARCHMENT PAPER is relatively thick and strong at 150gsm. It is easy to handle and therefore ideal for a beginner. It is suited to creating items such as boxes or bookmarks that require the paper to hold its shape. Either side of this paper can be used.

PARCHMENT VELLUMS are thinner at 90gsm. Although they come in a variety of colours and patterns, they are still translucent. With the patterned vellums, check which is the right side – the colour will be stronger and brighter on this side. Some highly patterned parchment vellums are unsuitable for embossing but they are ideal for background purposes.

Both parchment paper and vellum can be printed onto using a home computer and printer prior to embossing. This is an ideal way to add a personalized message (follow the manufacturers' instructions on both using the printer and paper).

Basic Techniques Tracing and Embossing

You will always need to begin with this basic technique in parchment craft. Your chosen design has first to be traced onto the parchment paper before being embossed. Designs can be embossed from just one side of the paper or both sides.

TRACING

It is important to take time and care over tracing a design, as this is the foundation from which you will emboss and produce your finished work. As you gain experience and confidence, you can draw freehand directly onto the parchment paper with a pencil and create your own designs.

Use a firm surface for the best result, and check that it is free from dirt and grease. First of all, you will need to decide whether to trace your design using white pencil, white ink or even a combination of both. Using white pencil is the most failsafe method for beginners.

WHITE PENCIL

- Pencil marks will rub off, so if you make a mistake in tracing your design, it can be easily corrected.
- Embossing over white pencil marks will not spoil the design.
- White pencil will blend into the design, creating a subtle outline.
- Make sure that your pencil is sharp, but avoid pressing too hard or you may scratch the surface of the paper and you won't be able to rub out any mistakes.

WHITE INK

- Tracings made with white ink will remain on the paper and so become part of the design.
- Ink creates a distinct outline to the design.
- For fine white lines, let the nib of the pen glide over the paper; for thicker lines, press harder as you trace.
- If you emboss over the top of a white ink line, it will become a shiny grey colour as it reacts to the metal tool. To avoid this problem, you can trace using white ink, then turn the paper over and emboss from the other side.

ALSO . . .

- Don't be afraid to turn the paper around as you trace, but keep it in line with the design underneath.
- Coloured or metallic inks can also be used.

The left-hand portion of the butterfly has been traced with white ink and the right-hand portion with white pencil.

EMBOSSING

The key to embossing is the pressure applied with the tool – less pressure produces light white marks; more pressure creates strong white marks. With a fine ball embossing tool, pressure is concentrated to a smaller area and strong lines can be made. There is more danger of tearing the paper with a fine ball tool, so take care. Strong lines can also be achieved with larger ball tools. These are ideal for embossing a large area evenly.

Always work your design from pale white to strong white – you can make a line stronger by applying more pressure, but once embossed, you can't go back.

To begin, position the parchment paper reverse-side up over the foam pad. You may need to rub the tool lightly over the area several times before you notice a change in the paper – this is normal and means that the tool and the paper are warming up.

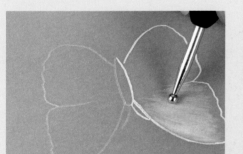

1 Emboss the design from the reverse side using the large ball embossing tool. Gently rub the large ball embossing tool in a side-to-side motion over the area you wish to become whiter.

2 Continue embossing until the paper is beginning to turn white. Keep turning over your paper to see how the right side is progressing – what you see from the back can be different from the front.

PRESSURE
Beware of using too much pressure. Above, the large and fine ball embossing tools were used with increasing amounts of pressure until the paper tore.

Project # Butterfly Card

This elegant, contemporary greetings card design features the technique of embossing in its traditional form, using a white pencil tracing on white parchment paper, but it is set off by a colourful card mount. Different sizes of embossing tool and varying amounts of pressure are employed to achieve the variations in tone. The fragile, paper-like qualities of butterfly wings are perfectly replicated by the fine tracery of the embossing lines.

You will need

white pencil

★

150 gsm plain parchment paper
11 x 24cm (4¼ x 9½in)

★

foam pad

★

fine ball embossing tool

★

large ball embossing tool

★

medium ball embossing tool

★

PVA (white) glue

★

purple single-fold card
12.5cm (4⅞in) square

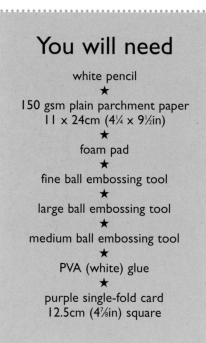

This project is ideal for a birthday or wedding card. The parchment paper can be printed before the project is begun with 'Happy Birthday' or 'Congratulations' to make it extra special.

1 Using the white pencil, draw a faint line widthways down the middle of the piece of parchment paper, to divide it into halves. One section will be the front of the card and the other the back. With the pencil, trace the butterflies and flowers from the template on page 130 onto the left-hand section of the parchment paper.

2 Place the parchment paper with the pencil tracing uppermost over your foam pad – remember that this is the reverse side. Emboss all the butterfly and flower outlines you have just drawn using the fine ball embossing tool and applying moderate pressure. If too much pressure is applied, the lines will become too prominent for the desired result. Turn the parchment paper over and check the other side to see if all the lines have been embossed.

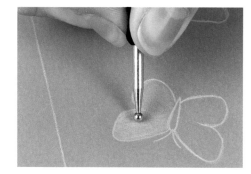

3 Start with butterfly A. With the pencil marks still uppermost, using the large ball embossing tool, gently start to emboss the wings, applying light strokes. Work from the wing tip to the centre backwards and forwards over the whole wing area. As this action warms the fibres and the tool, the paper will gradually begin to change colour.

4 Using a fine ball embossing tool, add the detail of the lines in the butterfly's wings, applying a little more pressure than previously. Continue with the same tool to fill in the butterfly's body. Turn the paper over and check that the embossing is even on both wings.

5 To make the wings a stronger white at the tips, use the medium ball embossing tool to emboss the edges, pressing gently to begin with until you can judge how the paper is responding. Aim for the effect of the strong white gradually fading to lighter white.

6 For butterfly B, using the large ball tool, emboss the wings starting from the body and working outwards to the wing tips, again using a backwards and forwards motion. Continue embossing until you have a light, even white all over the wings. Add the detail to the wings with the fine ball tool, pressing quite hard across the wings to create patches of strong white. Use the same tool to make the body a strong white.

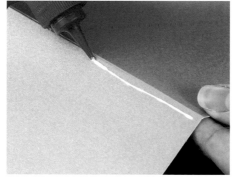

7 For butterfly C, emboss the wings following the instructions in Step 6, but this time apply more pressure near the body and less towards the wing tips, so that the stronger white at the body fades to a lighter white at the wing tips. Periodically turn the paper over to check the effect on the right side. Add the detail with the fine ball tool as in Step 6.

8 Fold the parchment paper in half along the pencil line you drew at the start. Run a fine line of PVA (white) glue along the back of the card near to the spine. Attach the parchment paper to the card – the glue will dry clear but still be visible through the paper, so take care not to get glue on the front of the card.

Further Technique Mounting

Mounting parchment paper onto card requires consideration – even clear glue shows through the translucent paper. Try out different-coloured background card to see which of these options works best with your design.

A Using greetings cards with apertures is an effective way to avoid this problem, fixing the design to the inside with double-sided adhesive tape.

B Another solution is to adhere the parchment paper to the spine of the card only, in which case allow in the size of the paper for it to be folded round the back of the card. See also Step 8, above.

C Alternatively, you could sew the paper into the spine of the card using a needle and thread.

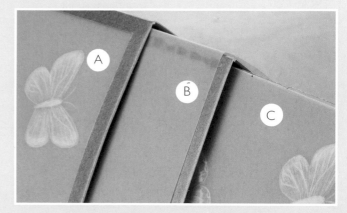

Further Techniques Pricking and Cutting

Pricking or perforating and cutting the parchment paper offer ways of bringing added interest and variety to parchment craft designs. For instance, a pricked border makes a dainty frame for an embossed motif, while pricked and then cut-out tiny sections of paper can create a delicate lace-like pattern as part of a design. The variations in these effects not only come from the particular tools used but also how much pressure is applied with the tool – needle tools can pierce right through the paper or just indent the surface.

Basic Tool Kit

SINGLE NEEDLE TOOL
This is the simplest pricking tool, in that it has only one sharp needle point.

TWO-NEEDLE TOOL
This tool has two needles side by side.

FOUR-NEEDLE TOOL
The four needles are set in a square formation so that when the paper is pricked the holes form an exact square.

FOAM PAD
An important part of the tool kit, it allows the paper to 'give' when embossing. Pads specially designed for parchment craft can be purchased but a piece of dark-coloured craft foam is ideal.

PUNCH WHEEL TOOL
The head of this tool has a rotating disk with spikes which, when wheeled along the paper, creates indents in the paper at regular intervals.

SCISSORS
A good-quality pair with fine-pointed blades are needed to cut out small sections of parchment paper that have first been pierced with needle tools.

Paper

Any parchment paper or vellum can be used, but the thicker variety of parchment paper is easier to handle. Parchment paper can be pricked from both sides, just as in paper pricking (see page 86).

PRICKING

Using a white pencil, trace the design onto tracing paper. Place it on top of the parchment paper. Using a two-needle tool, prick through both pieces of paper. Grids are available for placing over the parchment and pricking through with a single-needle tool.

CUTTING

Using a four-needle tool, prick right the way through the parchment paper. Insert the tips of finely pointed scissors and carefully cut away the paper in the middle of the four holes. This allows the colour of the background paper to show through, creating a lace-like effect.

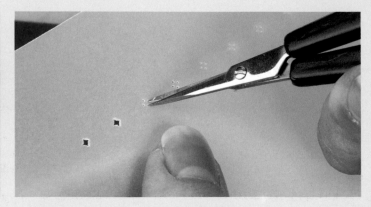

Further Technique Colour

Colour can be added to parchment paper to give it an extra dimension. Areas such as borders can be left plain white to complement a colourful image in the centre of a card. Colour can be applied prior to embossing or, once the colour has dried, you can emboss from the other side of the paper. You may find a preferred method of applying colour to parchment, or try using a combination of several methods. Take time to experiment first on a scrap piece of parchment paper.

Paper

It is best to use 150gsm plain parchment paper for painting or colouring. Colour can be applied to both sides of the paper, although using the right side of the paper will create a more vibrant effect. When using felt-tip pens or watercolour pencils in particular, you will need to judge carefully how much is needed to be properly absorbed by the paper but not too much otherwise the paper will start to buckle.

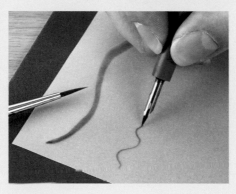

FELT-TIP PENS

Felt-tip pens can be applied direct to parchment paper for producing strong colours. You can also rub a felt-tip pen onto a ceramic dish and then use a fine, damp paintbrush to pick up the colour and apply to the paper. The dish can also be used as a palette for mixing colours. As packs of felt-tip pens are inexpensive, this is a really good method for a beginner.

INKS

Specialist parchment craft inks can be bought in a range of colours which can be applied straight from the bottle. They can also be diluted with water to produce lighter colours or mixed together to make additional colours. The inks can be applied with a mapping pen or a damp paintbrush. Shake the ink bottle well before using the ink, especially metallic inks. Most of these inks are water resistant once dry, but follow the manufacturer's instructions.

WATERCOLOUR PENCILS

Watercolour pencils are used like any colouring pencil to colour, shade or outline a design. However, the difference is that watercolour pencils allow you to go over the area you have coloured with a damp paintbrush and blend the colour. Layers of colour can be built up and subtle tones achieved. Watercolour pencils come in a range of colours and are easy to use.

OIL PASTELS

Oil pastels are in a separate category because they are not water based. They therefore need a medium such as white spirit to apply the colour and for cleaning brushes after use. Take extra care when using mediums such as white spirit as they are highly flammable. Oil pastels can be applied direct to the parchment paper and then blended using a paintbrush or kitchen paper. They are more expensive than felt-tip pens or watercolour pencils and take a little more time to become accustomed to using.

Project Teddy Picture

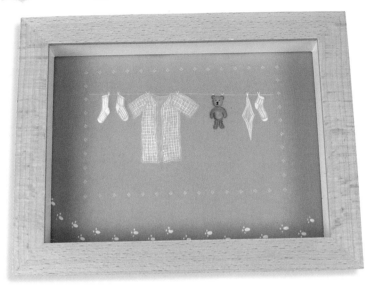

The cute teddy in this plain parchment-embossed design is highlighted on the washing line using blended colour from a watercolour pencil. The design is further enhanced by a paw-print border along the bottom, pricked out of the parchment paper. Suitably framed, this endearing picture would make an ideal gift for a christening or a child's birthday.

You will need

white pencil
★
150gsm plain parchment paper
20 x 15cm (8 x 6in)
★
foam pad
★
embossing tools:
fine ball, medium ball and large ball
★
ruler
★
punch wheel tool
★
brown watercolour pencil
★
paintbrush and jar of water
★
kitchen paper
★
black pen
★
tracing paper
20 x 15cm (8 x 6in)
★
low-tack adhesive tape (optional)
★
four-needle tool
★
blue card
★
photo frame

1 Using a white pencil, trace the teddy design, except the border, from the template on page 131, onto the parchment paper. Place the paper with the pencil tracing uppermost over the foam pad. Using the fine ball embossing tool, gently emboss the straight washing line with a ruler. Emboss the outlines of the teddy and all the items on the line, leaving the paw prints until later.

2 Using the medium ball embossing tool, emboss the socks all over. Add the line detail with the fine ball embossing tool. Repeat for the handkerchief.

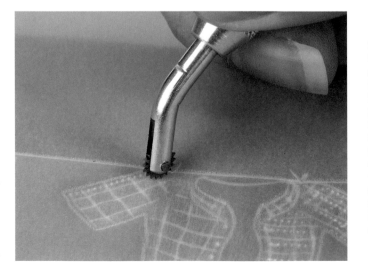

3 Using the large ball embossing tool, gently emboss the shirt all over to achieve a light white. Remember to turn the paper over periodically to check the other side. Gently add lines using the medium ball embossing tool. Using the punch wheel tool, add the lines to the shirt, or use the fine ball tool to add a line of dots over the shirt.

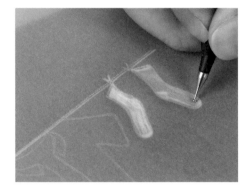

4 Turn the parchment paper over so that you are working on the right side. Using a brown watercolour pencil, outline the teddy, then colour in the rest of the teddy. Use a damp paintbrush to blend the colour. Turn the paper over and use the large ball tool to gently emboss the teddy's face and tummy. Turn the paper back to the right side and add the facial details to the teddy with a black pen.

5 Trace the border from the template on page 131 onto tracing paper. With the parchment paper over the foam pad and the design uppermost, place the tracing over the parchment paper and hold in place with your spare hand or use low-tack adhesive tape. Using the tour-needle tool, prick through the tracing paper to the parchment paper every 1cm (⅜in) where marked.

6 Once the border is complete, turn the parchment paper over so that the design is face down on the foam pad. Using the medium ball tool, emboss the paw prints with a circular motion. Don't worry if the paw prints are not identical – they look more effective when they are slightly irregular. To display, mount the design in a photo frame with blue card behind it to give the background colour.

When embossing the border, use a spare piece of paper on which to rest your hand while working to protect the work you have already done.

Project Floral Garland Card

This dainty card design, suitable for marking all kinds of special occasions, combines several parchment craft techniques. The gold flower stem adds a luxurious touch and perfectly complements the delicate pink blooms.

You will need

pencil and tracing paper
★
parchment paper
12 x 6cm (4¾ x 2⅜in)
★
low-tack adhesive tape
★
mapping pen and gold parchment ink
★
scrap paper
★
white pencil
★
foam pad
★
felt-tip pens in two shades of pink
★
saucer, jar of water and fine paintbrush
★
embossing tools:
medium ball and fine ball
★
fine needle and pink cotton
★
blue metallic single-fold card
14 x 8cm (5½ x 3¼in)
★
scissors

1 Trace the design from the template on page 130 onto tracing paper. Place the parchment paper over the tracing and hold in place with low-tack adhesive tape. Dip the mapping pen in gold ink and, with one stroke of the pen, trace over the central stalk of the flower. Practise first on scrap paper. Trace the flowers and stems in gold ink.

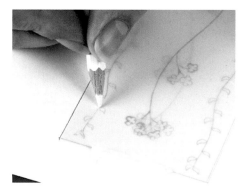

2 When the ink is thoroughly dry, turn the parchment paper over and secure in place on the tracing with low-tack adhesive tape. Using a white pencil, trace over the two rows of leaves.

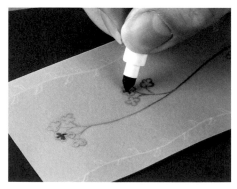

3 Remove the tape and the tracing. Place the parchment paper, gold inked-side up, over a foam pad so that the dark background allows you to see what you are doing. Using a pink felt-tip pen, colour the central flower in each cluster. Don't colour over the gold lines.

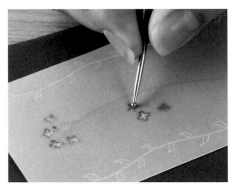

4 Rub one of the pink felt-tip pens onto the saucer several times so that a residue of pink ink is left. Pick up the ink with a damp paintbrush and colour in a flower. Colour in the remaining flowers, picking up more ink each time.

5 When the flowers have dried, turn the parchment paper over, keeping it on the foam pad. Using a medium ball embossing tool, lightly emboss all the flowers.

This design can be easily adapted to a different size of card by adding more flowers to the central stem.

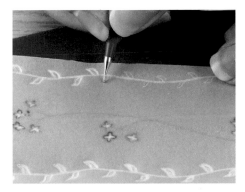

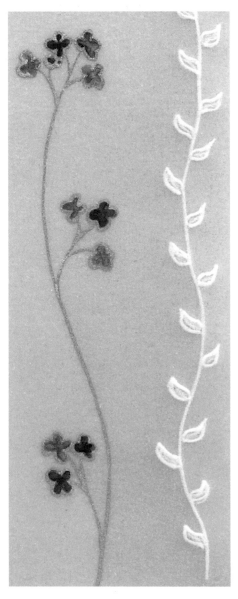

6 Using the fine ball embossing tool, emboss the two long stalks of the leaves. Outline the leaves and add a central vein to each leaf (see detail, right).

7 Using a fine needle threaded with pink cotton, sew the parchment paper to the front of the single-fold card with a stitch in each corner. Tie the ends of the cotton on the back of the card and trim.

Pricking

The techniques for pricking originate from around the 18th century, and probably have not changed since that time. Using a pin or needle, small holes are pricked into a piece of paper to create a design – and that's it! The appeal of this craft is in its simplicity, and anyone can achieve great results in no time at all.

A needle pushed into a cork is all you need to get going with this craft, but you can use anything that will pierce a hole in paper. If you have parchment-pricking tools, such as the four-needle tool used for the Teddy Picture on pages 82–83, you could also use these for paper pricking. Any paper can be used for pricking and the design can be pricked from either side. The pricked holes can form a motif, a pattern for a border, lettering or all three combined. A wide variety of ready-made templates are now available for creating all kinds of designs for every occasion.

Basic Tool Kit

NEEDLE AND CORK
Any ordinary sewing needle can be used, but don't use a tapestry needle. You will need a dense cork in which to mount the needle, otherwise the needle will be pushed down into cork when pressure is applied. (If you enjoy this technique, it is worth investing in a special needle vice – it is easier to handle than a cork.)

METAL TEMPLATES
These are patterns ready-cut especially for pricking. The paper is placed underneath, and the pattern pricked through the holes in the template to the paper below. Not all the design has to be pricked, and by using different elements of the template, variations of a single design can be achieved. Choose templates with a variety of designs so that you can mix and match images or patterns.

FOAM PAD
This allows the needle to be pushed fully through the paper and also protects your work surface from the needle point as you work.

Paper

Any paper in which you can pierce a hole with a needle can be used, but test how the design shows up before embarking on a whole project. As the needle pierces the paper, it pushes up raised edges around the hole and these cast a shadow. On darker papers, these shadows are lost, so the design may not be visible enough.

Basic Technique

Different effects can be achieved with a single-sized needle by simply applying varying amounts of pressure, so that the holes vary from fine indentations on the surface of the paper (right-hand row) to holes fully pierced through the paper (left-hand row). Alternatively, you can use needles of different sizes to vary the size of the indents and holes produced. Pricking a combination of both sides (i.e. pricking from the back of the paper in places) brings added textural interest to the design (middle row).

Effective border patterns can be created by pricking holes closely together in a line so that the paper is almost cut out. When pricking designs, work systematically to make sure that no parts of the design are missed.

USING A SEWING MACHINE
Use the patterns on a sewing machine to make speedy but fancy shapes. Take care as paper will quickly blunt needles.

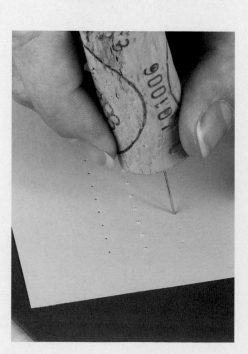

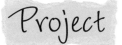
Project # Fern Panels

In this graphic, elegant greetings card project, pricking is used to define the leaf motif. The design could also be adapted for use as a border in a photo frame.

A message could be pricked onto the middle panel, but if pricking from the wrong side, the letters need to be in reverse.

You will need

pencil
★
tracing paper
★
two pieces of green paper
3 × 6.5cm (1⅛ × 2½in)
★
foam pad
★
low-tack adhesive tape (optional)
★
needle and cork
★
pale green paper
3 × 6.5cm (1⅛ × 2½in)
★
translucent green parchment paper
10 × 14cm (4 × 5½in)
★
dark green card
11.5 × 15.5cm (4½ × 6in)
with an aperture
8 × 12.5cm (3¼ × 4⅞in)
★
double-sided adhesive tape
★
PVA (white) glue

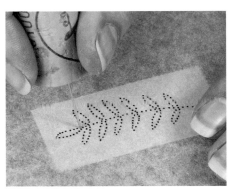

1 Trace the design from the template on page 130 onto tracing paper. Place one piece of the green paper over the foam pad, then place the tracing on top of the green paper. Secure the tracing to the paper with low-tack adhesive tape or just hold it in place with your spare hand. Prick the outline of the leaf design with the needle and cork, following the dots for evenly spaced holes, piercing both the tracing and green paper.

3 Attach the translucent green parchment paper to the inside of the aperture of the dark green card using double-sided adhesive tape. Using PVA (white) glue, stick the three pricked leaf designs to the parchment paper, ensuring that they are evenly spaced.

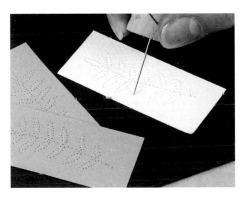

2 Remove the tracing paper and turn the green paper over. Add a line of fine pricks with the needle to the centres of each of the leaves. Use gentle pricks close together so that the paper is not pierced all the way through. Repeat to prick the design onto the second piece of green paper and the pale green paper.

Embossing

This is where a raised image is made, on a single piece of paper, by applying pressure. The fibres of the paper are stretched to make a new shape but the colour does not change, as it does in parchment craft (see pages 76–85). Paper embossing relies on the shadows created by the raised edges of the design to define the image. This is why letters are particularly suited to embossing. The craft became popular in Victorian times, when writing paper and envelopes were decoratively embossed.

To emboss paper requires a stencil, or a mould, where areas are cut out allowing the paper to be pressed and therefore stretched into these cutout areas. Pre-cut metal stencils are available for this craft, but you can also be inventive and make your own.

Basic Tool Kit

EMBOSSING TOOLS
The size of the smooth metal ball attached to the handle varies. A medium and large ball embossing tool are recommended. Embossing tools used for parchment craft can also be used for paper embossing.

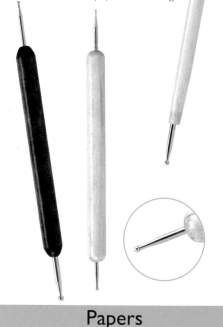

LIGHTBOX
A light source is required when using stencils as the paper is placed over the stencil. Without light behind, it can be difficult to see the design to emboss. Lightboxes can be relatively inexpensive and are a good investment. They consist of a light bulb underneath a plastic box, which allows you to work over the box with the light coming from under the stencil. If you don't want to invest in a lightbox initially, you can use a window as a light source. However, it is quite difficult to hold the paper and stencil in place while embossing.

EMBOSSING STENCILS
Metal stencils are available for embossing in a variety of patterns. As with other stencils, choose carefully when purchasing. Some embossing stencils have borders or a whole image already cut out, so they are ready for you to use straight away. Not all of the design on a stencil has to be embossed and this allows you to gain more from your stencils by bringing together elements of several stencils.

Papers

Thinner papers are easier to use for paper embossing; if the paper is too thick, it is hard to emboss as the fibres cannot be easily distorted. Handmade papers are generally too textured for embossing, although there may be some with a finer texture that might work. Smooth machine-made papers show the embossed design to best effect. Light-coloured papers are preferable – the shadows cast by the embossing tend to be lost on darker-coloured paper.

Basic Technique

The size of embossing tool required will depend on the size of the pattern on the stencil you are using. Smaller patterns will require the medium ball embossing tool, whereas with other stencils you may find that just using the large ball embossing tool is easier. The weight of paper will influence how hard you need to press with the tools. With heavier papers, you may need to dampen them prior to embossing. This can be done with extreme care, by holding the paper near to the steam from a boiling kettle. Hold the paper with clean, plastic tongs to protect your hands from the steam. It is possible to emboss both sides of the same piece of paper in order to create more contrast.

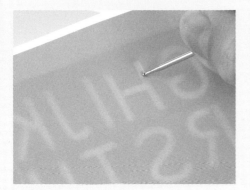

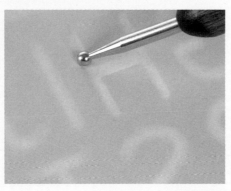

1 Place the stencil on the lightbox. If you are using letters or numbers, the stencil needs to be placed wrong-side down so that they are back to front. Place your paper over the top of the stencil. If the paper has a right and wrong side, it needs to be wrong-side down for the raised image to appear on the right side. Press into the edges of the stencil with the medium ball embossing tool, in order to outline the image.

2 Use the large ball embossing tool to emboss the inner areas.

EMBOSSING PRESSURE
The letter on the left did not have enough pressure applied with the embossing tool. If this occurs, line up the template with the design and go over it again with the tool. The middle letter is embossed with the correct amount of pressure, but too much pressure was applied to the letter on the right, causing the paper to tear.

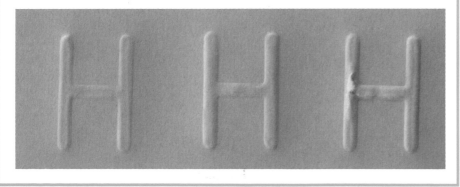

Project Classical Wedding Stationery

This elegant gift bag, card and envelope and place name cards are all embossed to make a complete set of handcrafted wedding stationery. In this project, a single embossing stencil was used in three different ways to offer variations on the basic design while retaining a coordinated look.

You will need

GIFT BAG
purple giftwrap 18 x 30cm (7 x 12in)
★
pieces of wood or a box to use as a mould 5cm (2in) deep x 8cm (3¼in) wide and more than 13cm (5in) long
★
double-sided adhesive tape (optional)
★
hole punch
★
green ribbon 30cm (12in) long

CARD AND ENVELOPE
2 pieces of green giftwrap
20 x 2.5cm (8 x 1in) and
23 x 17cm (9 x 6¾in)
★
cream single-fold card 10cm (4in) square

PLACE NAME CARD
green giftwrap 9 x 2cm (3½ x ¾in)
★
cream card 5 x 10cm (2 x 4in)

FOR ALL
metal embossing stencil
(see page 88)
★
lightbox
★
large ball embossing tool
★
glue stick

1 Place the stencil on the lightbox. Place the piece of purple giftwrap right-side down centrally over the stencil. Using the large ball embossing tool, emboss the larger square with the dashed outline of the design.

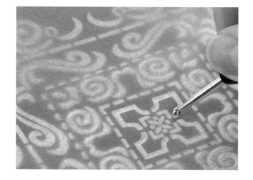

2 Turn the paper over and line up the square you have embossed with the square on the stencil. Emboss the central square with the cross only using the large ball embossing tool.

3 Remove the paper from the stencil and turn the lightbox off. Fold over 2cm (¾in) along the top edge of the paper. Place the paper on the mould, making sure that the motif you have embossed is central to the mould and 3cm (1⅛in) of paper is extending from the bottom edge. Fold the paper around the mould. Complete the gift bag following the instructions on page 17 – use double-sided adhesive tape instead of a glue stick if the paper is shiny, as here, and will not hold the glue. Punch a hole either side at the top of the bag, thread the ribbon through and tie in a bow.

CARD AND ENVELOPE

1 Place the 20 x 2.5cm (8 x 1in) piece of green giftwrap over the stencil on the lightbox and, by moving the paper over the stencil and selecting areas of the design, emboss three swirls and four leaf shapes onto the paper strip with the large ball embossing tool. Glue the strip around the cream single-fold card.

2 Cut an envelope from the remaining piece of giftwrap using the template on page 127. Place right-side down over the metal stencil. Using the large ball embossing tool, emboss large swirls all over the paper. Remove the paper from the stencil and the lightbox. Make up the envelope following the instructions on page 16.

Multiples of this card and envelope could be used either as invitations or as thank you cards by adding appropriate text to the fronts of the cards.

PLACE NAME CARD

1 Place the green giftwrap over the stencil on the lightbox with the leaf motif you are about to emboss 3cm (1⅛in) from the top of the paper. Using the large ball embossing tool, emboss the leaf and swirl.

2 Move the piece of paper down the stencil to the lower leaf shape. Emboss the motif using the large ball embossing tool. Glue the embossed strip around the cream card 1cm (⅜in) from the left-hand edge.

Mix & Match

Parchment-Packaged Pot Pourri

A sheet of parchment paper was embossed with a butterfly and flower design, and the top edge trimmed with fancy-edged scissors. The paper was then scored according to the dimensions of the box used as a mould (see page 17). This resulted in crisp edges to the gift bag when it was assembled. It was then filled with pot pourri.

Vintage Celebration

Grapes and leaves were first embossed onto parchment paper. Burgundy-coloured card was then folded in half and cut into a wine bottle shape. A rectangular aperture was cut in the bottle shape and embossed parchment paper mounted behind the aperture. Blue paper was glued to the top, embellished with gold pen. A message or greeting could be added to look like part of the wine label, either to mark a special wedding anniversary or a birthday.

Pricked Patchwork

Squares of pink and blue papers were pricked with hearts, flowers and swirls, then arranged on blue handmade paper to fit the size of the lid of this ready-made box. The papers were then stitched onto the blue paper using a sewing machine and gold thread (see pages 28–31) and the paper attached to the lid. You could make your own gift box following the instructions on page 18. For a quicker alternative, glue the pricked motifs to the lid rather than sewing them.

Personally Presented

Just a few minutes spent decorating an envelope makes all the difference. The envelope shape was cut out (template on page 127) and then pricked using a needle mounted in a cork. The letter A, with a simple border, was used to embellish the front, with the pattern continuing onto the flap. The envelope was then assembled (see page 16). As an alternative, hearts were pricked into a strip of paper, which was then glued to the front of an envelope. These envelopes are not suitable for posting.

Alphabet Embossing

The letters A, B and C were embossed onto squares of coloured paper. These were then mounted onto a single-fold green card. A strip of embossed letters glued across the bottom of the card adds a final flourish. Alternatively, you could emboss the initials of the recipient of the card.

Panelled Parchment

Flowers were cut from parchment paper and embossed, resulting in the edges of the petals curling. Yellow felt-tip pen was used to colour the centres of the flowers, which were then attached to a starkly-contrasting deep red card. Two panels of embossed leaves were added either side of the flowers. A greeting could be added to the card in place of the central flower.

Floral Frieze Bookmark

A delicate flower pattern was embossed onto a strip of parchment paper, then placed inside a green two-fold bookmark. A hole was punched in the top and a coordinating-coloured tassel threaded through. You could also use the design for the Floral Garland Card on pages 84–85 to make a bookmark in the same way.

Printing & Presenting

RUBBER STAMPING • SCRAPBOOKING

Rubber Stamping has brought simple printing methods into the craft arena and made them accessible to all. The amazing range of designs and inkpads available makes stamping such an enticing and popular craft. Scrapbooking, with its art of organizing and embellishing photos, also has universal application and instant appeal. Beginners and the experienced alike will benefit from the 'back to basics' approach in this chapter. Sound guidance is given to help you make an informed choice from the bewildering array of products on offer. The techniques involved are also given a fresh focus — in stamping, the emphasis is on getting the most from your stamps by using them in unexpected ways, while in scrapbooking, the underlying principles of effectively composing and framing pictures are explored. The Mix & Match examples prove that, although stamping is such a speedy way of producing cards and packaging, it doesn't mean a compromise on quality or design.

Clockwise from left: Leaf Writing Paper and Envelopes, pages 98–99; Traveller's Companion, page 110; Silver-Leaf Gift Box, page 111; Daisy and Butterfly Card, pages 102–103; Gilded Heart Giftwrap, page 105; Portrait in Pink Scrapbook Page, pages 108–109

Rubber Stamping

This is the technique of printing a design using a rubber stamp. Rubber stamping is a relatively new papercraft but it has become so popular that it is probably the most widely practised. Now abbreviated to 'stamping', its popularity has resulted in a fantastic range of products and thousands of rubber stamps to choose from.

The design is pre-cut into rubber and mounted on a wooden block, making it easy to handle. The stamp is inked using an inkpad, then pressed onto paper, transferring the design to the paper. This means that one design can be printed over and over again, with each print identical. The professional look that the rubber stamp gives an item, while retaining its essential handmade quality, is the appeal of this papercraft.

Basic Tool Kit

STAMPS
Stamps come in all shapes and sizes. They have a design cut into a layer of rubber, which is then mounted onto a wooden block or foam pad. Stamps mounted on wood are more expensive but easier to handle.

Outline stamps
These print only the outline of the image, leaving blank areas which can then be coloured in.

Solid stamps These print the image as a block, without leaving any blank areas to be coloured in.

INKPADS
Inkpads have a felt pad in which the ink is stored. They may be a single colour or multicoloured. They come in a variety of sizes and are therefore not the same size and shape as your stamp.

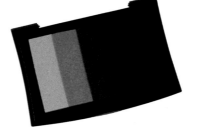

Dye-based inkpads These are water based, ready to use and fast drying. They are suitable for use on most papers but they may bleed a little on absorbent papers. They come in a range of colours, from vivid to softer tones. Some of these pads offer several colours in one pad. Dye-based inkpads are not suitable for embossing.

Embossing inkpads See Embossing, page 104, for information on these inkpads and their application.

DUAL-TIP PENS
Pens are available for stamping that have a fine tip at one end and a brush tip at the other. The stamp is inked by using the dual-tip pen directly on the stamp. The advantage of using these pens is that you can apply several colours to one stamp.

DUAL-TIP SPONGE DABBERS
These have a sponge either end in which the ink is stored. The stamp is inked by dabbing the sponge onto the stamp.

Papers

Any paper can be stamped but textured paper will not result in an even print – but this may be the effect that you want to achieve. Fine papers such as tissue or mulberry papers absorb the ink and the image will be blurred. Always test a stamp by printing on a scrap piece of the paper or card that you are planning to use before embarking on a project.

Basic Technique

These basic guidelines will get you started with stamping. By following this simple advice, you will achieve a good, clean printed image or design every time.

INKING AND PRINTING

1 Inkpads are often smaller than the stamp, but this is not a problem. Rather than applying the stamp to the inkpad, do the reverse. Hold the stamp in one hand, design uppermost. Take a single-colour inkpad in the other hand and dab it over the design. Dab several times so that the whole surface is covered with ink. When using multicoloured inkpads, do not dab the inkpad over the image or the colours will be mixed and muddied. Instead, firmly press the inkpad once onto the stamp leaving a range of colours on the stamp.

2 An even coat of ink is left on the stamp. Note how no ink has touched the edge of the rubber or the wooden block. If ink does get on the surrounding rubber or wood, it is best to wipe it off carefully with a piece of kitchen paper before printing, particularly if there is ink on the surrounding rubber, as this may transfer to the paper when printed.

3 It is important to work on a perfectly flat surface. Position the stamp over the paper but not touching. Press the stamp onto the paper in an even manner. Lift the stamp off immediately and take care not to smudge the print. You may want to hold the paper down with the other hand when removing a stamp. You can now print the stamp again without inking up and a lighter image will be printed. This technique of fading out is very effective and can give an extra spatial dimension, as the lighter images retreat into the background.

FOR SHARP RESULTS
When inking a stamp, avoid dragging the inkpad over the stamp, and don't rock the stamp on the paper when printing, or this will smudge the print.

STAMPING KIT CARE

With all types of inkpads, pens and dabbers, replace the lids immediately after use or they will dry out. All stamps need to be cleaned after use, and they should also be cleaned during a project if you are using more than one colour. Place two pieces of damp kitchen paper in a saucer and press the stamp into the paper several times. Dry the stamp with clean, dry kitchen paper. Never immerse stamps in water.

Once the stamp is clean, it should be stored away from sunlight and heat, otherwise the rubber may perish. Try to store stamps with the design uppermost. Inkpads are best stored upside down so that the ink runs to the surface of the foam pad.

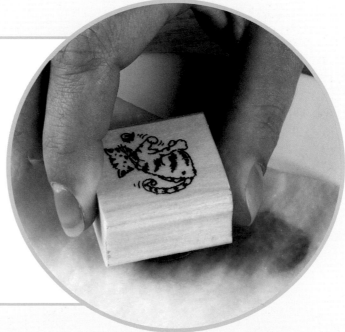

Project Leaf Writing Paper and Envelopes

Stamping is such an easy way to make a letter extra special, yet only one stamp was used to create this complete look. Why not continue the design onto the envelope for a complete handcrafted look.

1 Place a piece of scrap paper under a sheet of writing paper. Place another piece of torn scrap paper over the right-hand two-thirds of the writing paper so that only the left-hand third is visible. Hold in place with small pieces of low-tack adhesive tape. Ink the stamp using the green inkpad. Stamp twice onto the remaining piece of scrap paper. Print onto the top of the writing paper. Turn the stamp at an angle and print again below. Print again at the bottom of the paper. The leaf print will fade with each print made, but it will remain quite clear.

2 Ink the stamp again and print onto scrap paper once. Print onto the writing paper but this time print over the edge of the torn scrap paper. Print again three times over the top, left and bottom of the writing paper, turning the stamp at different angles each time you print and making sure that you print over the edges.

You will need

three large pieces of scrap paper
★
cream writing paper
18 x 14cm (7 x 5½in)
and matching envelopes
★
low-tack adhesive tape
★
green dye-based inkpad
★
solid leaf stamp

3 Ink the stamp but don't print onto scrap paper. Align the edges of the stamp with the top left-hand corner of the writing paper and print. Ink the stamp again and print onto the writing paper below the leaf just printed. Now you have two darker leaf prints on a background of lighter green prints.

4 Using the same technique, print the front of an envelope with the leaf design. Turn the envelope over, ink the stamp and print along the centre of the envelope over the flap. Without re-inking the stamp, print either side of this initial print. Leave spaces between the leaves, or overlap them as shown in the finished picture.

Further Technique ALIGNING STAMPS

Rulers are available that allow you to line up your stamps when printing, but it is possible to improvise with a piece of wood. You will need a 20cm (8in) length of clean wood 2 x 4cm (¾ x 1½in).

1 Using a pencil, mark the length of the stamp on the width and depth of the wood. Print the stamp you want to line up onto tracing paper. While the stamp is still on the tracing paper, draw around it in pencil. Place the tracing paper image where you want the print to appear. Align the marks on the wood with those on the tracing paper.

2 Slide the tracing paper out without moving the piece of wood. Ink the stamp, line it up with the pencil marks and print. You can now repeat this procedure to create a perfectly straight line of prints.

PRODUCTION LINES
This is an ideal opportunity to set up a mini production line to produce a whole set of stationery. Instead of printing onto scrap paper first, print onto the envelope or another sheet of writing paper, to consolidate your efforts.

Further Technique COLOURING IN

With outline stamps, there are blank areas within the image for you to colour in. Colour can be added using felt-tip pens, colouring pencils or watercolour pencils.

FELT-TIP PENS

These pens produce stronger, darker colours than colouring pencils or watercolour pencils. They are best used to colour in small areas of a print – on larger areas, you are liable to leave streaks in the colour.

COLOURING PENCILS

Ordinary colouring pencils can be used to colour or shade any rubber-stamped design. Colouring pencils come in a wide range of types and prices, but it is best to invest in good-quality pencils.

WATERCOLOUR PENCILS

Watercolour pencils can be used like any colouring pencil to colour or shade a design. The colour is then blended using a damp paintbrush. The colours can be more vibrant, built up in layers and more subtle tones achieved than with ordinary colouring pencils. This motif was first embossed with gold embossing powder, then colour was applied with a watercolour pencil and blended with a damp paintbrush.

> **TESTING YOUR INKPAD**
> A dye-based inkpad should be used to print the outline, and it is advisable to test first on scrap paper in case the print bleeds when the damp paintbrush is used.

Felt-tip pens have been used to colour in a repeat stamped motif in three different ways. See Chorus Line, page 111.

Further Technique MASKING

This technique allows you to print overlapping images so that one image looks as if it is behind the other. However, this only works with stamps that have a simple outline which you will be able to cut out. This technique can be used with one stamp or it allows you to combine several different stamps for a project.

1 Print the design onto a stick-on note. Make sure that you print over part of the adhesive strip on the back of the stick-on note as this holds it in place later on. Cut out part, or all, of the design.

2 Print the design onto paper. Place the stick-on note exactly over the print on the paper. If you don't position it correctly first time, the advantage of using stick-on notes is that you can easily re-position them.

3 Ink your stamp again and print partially over the stick-on note. Remove the stick-on note and put it to one side. This stick-on note can then be used again and again in the same project or kept for future projects.

These pretty flowers, from page 102, have been stamped using masking, then coloured using slightly different shades of orange to give a subtle three-dimensional look.

MASKING LARGER IMAGES
For larger images, use a larger size of stick-on notes, but always ensure that you print over the adhesive strip.

VARYING COLOURS
The second image can be printed in a different colour to create a more interesting effect, but the stamp will need to cleaned first.

Daisy and Butterfly Card

This vibrant card design, involving masking and colouring in, will fascinate and delight everyone, as they try to work out how it was printed!

You will need

butterfly outline stamp
★
purple dye-based inkpad
★
stick-on notes
★
small scissors
★
flower outline stamp
★
yellow card 20 x 10cm (8 x 4in)
★
orange dye-based inkpad
★
orange, yellow and green watercolour pencils
★
jar of water and fine paintbrush
★
black, pink and blue felt-tip pens
★
pink single-fold card
18 x 8cm (7 x 3¼in)
★
small adhesive foam pads
★
light blue card 8 x 5cm (3¼ x 2in)

1 Use the purple inkpad, or any other strong colour, to print the butterfly image on a stick-on note and cut out. Print the flower on two stick-on notes and cut out both, leaving a small section – the adhesive part of the stick-on note – untrimmed.

2 Use the purple inkpad again to print the butterfly near the top of the yellow card. Place the stick-on note butterfly exactly over the printed butterfly on the yellow card.

3 Use the orange inkpad to ink the flower stamp. Print a flower directly over the butterfly stick-on note. Ink the stamp again and print another flower underneath the first flower, leaving a space between them. Repeat, then remove the butterfly stick-on note.

4 Place the two stick-on note flowers over the first two flowers. Ink the flower stamp and print a flower between the stick-on note flowers – the edges of the flowers should overlap. Remove the stick-on note from the top flower and place it over the bottom flower. Ink the stamp again and print another flower between these flowers. Remove the stick-on notes.

5 Using orange watercolour pencils, colour in the first three flowers that were printed. Use a damp paintbrush to blend the colours, to make them more vibrant. Using a yellow watercolour pencil, colour in the last two printed flowers and blend the colour with the paintbrush as before. Colour the centres of the flowers with yellow and a touch of green watercolour pencil.

6 Colour the body of the butterfly with the black felt-tip pen, then colour the wings of the butterfly with pink and blue felt-tip pens. Any colours can be used for the wings as long as they are vibrant.

7 Cut out the strip of flowers using a small pair of scissors. Mount on the right-hand edge of the pink single-fold card using adhesive foam pads. Print two butterflies onto the light blue card. Colour these in with felt-tip pens and cut out. Mount onto the card using small adhesive foam pads.

Butterfly and flower stamps are very popular, so if you have ones that are not the same as these, you can easily adapt this project to suit your own stamps.

Further Technique EMBOSSING

Embossing in the context of rubber stamping means something quite different than in relation to other papercrafts. Here, it refers to the technique of heating embossing powder, which then melts to become raised and shiny. Not all stamped designs are suitable for embossing, as the fine detail of the print is lost when the embossing powder melts.

Basic Tool Kit

EMBOSSING INKPADS
These are designed specifically for embossing and dry slowly.

WOODEN CLOTHES PEGS
Wooden clothes pegs are used to hold the paper when embossing to protect your hands from the heat of the heat gun. Do not use plastic clothes pegs as they will melt.

EMBOSSING POWDERS
These special loose powders for embossing come in a range of colours, with gold and silver metallics being very popular. They can only be used with pigment inkpads (see page 96) or embossing inkpads. Heat is directed over the powder, melting it into a semi-liquid state before drying solid.

EMBOSSING HEAT GUN
Embossing requires a heat source. While you can improvise with an iron to apply heat to the underside of the paper, it is highly recommended to invest in a heat gun. It directs heat to a small area, allowing you to control the embossing. The end of the heat gun gets very hot, so follow the manufacturer's instructions when using it. A heat gun is not a hairdryer, although some look very similar to one.

Follow these basic steps in order to emboss your stamp designs not only effectively but safely.

1 Using either a pigment or an embossing inkpad, ink your stamp design and print it onto paper. Sprinkle the embossing powder over the inked image while it is still wet. The embossing powder will stick to the areas of the paper that have been printed. Make sure that there is an even covering of powder.

2 Shake off the excess embossing powder onto a spare piece of paper. This powder can then be returned to the container and used again. Tap the printed paper gently to remove any specks of powder – if these are left, they will melt onto the paper. Use a fine paintbrush to remove any traces.

3 Holding the printed paper in one hand with a wooden peg, with the other hand, direct the heat gun onto the image, keeping it 15–20cm (6–8in) away from the paper. Watch the embossing powder melt to a semi-liquid form, then remove the heat gun and switch off. If the powder is over-heated, the image will not be glossy. The image can be left as it is or coloured in using any medium of your choice (see page 100).

Project Gilded Heart Giftwrap

Stamping is particularly suited to making stationery such as giftwrap and tags because it allows you to produce multiple identical images in a relatively short space of time. It can be extended to gift bags and boxes or other special-occasion stationery such as invitations, place name cards or thank you cards.

You will need

heart outline stamp
★
clear embossing inkpad
★
burgundy handmade paper
50 x 70cm (20 x 27½in)
★
gold embossing powder
★
large sheet of scrap paper
★
fine paintbrush
★
wooden clothes pegs
★
heat gun

With such a large sheet of paper, you need to make sure that you have enough embossing powder before you begin the project.

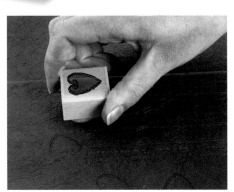

1 Use the heart stamp and clear embossing inkpad to print hearts randomly over the burgundy paper. If you want to do a section of the paper at a time, divide it into quarters and do Steps 1–3 for each quarter.

2 Sprinkle gold embossing powder over all the hearts, ensuring that they are entirely and evenly covered with powder. Shake off the excess powder onto scrap paper and return to the jar. Using a fine paintbrush, remove any specks of embossing powder left between the hearts.

To make the gift tag, a single heart was embossed in gold onto burgundy card. The hole for the gift tie was punched using a regular office hole punch.

3 Using wooden clothes pegs to hold the paper, melt the embossing powder on all the hearts with the heat gun. Leave the heat gun in a safe place to cool down.

Scrapbooking

Scrapbooks have existed since the 18th century, when ladies would fill journals with prints or 'scraps'. The pages would then be embellished with handwritten notes or verses. As photography became widespread, photographs were mounted onto the pages of these journals.

Today, scrapbooking is a broad term referring to the selection, arrangement and embellishing of photographs in an album. The craft of scrapbooking has become hugely popular, initially in the US and now in England and Europe, because it combines creativity with cataloguing photos, turning a chore into a rewarding pastime. The popularity of scrapbooking is also due to the rise of scrapbooking clubs, where families and friends get together in order to work on their own projects. This allows and encourages the sharing of ideas and techniques while having fun at the same time.

Basic Tool Kit

SCRAPBOOKS

A scrapbook is actually the same thing as a photo album. There are many scrapbooks available, but you get what you pay for. If you are going to invest a lot of time in this hobby, it is wise to invest in a good-quality scrapbook before you begin. Don't use a scrapbook with self-adhesive pages.

CORNER ROUNDER

This punch crops photos by punching out the outside edges. Place the photo in the corner rounder and press on it in the same way as a punch.

CUTTING TEMPLATES AND CUTTER

Templates of various shapes and sizes are used for cropping photographs. The template is placed over the photo, then the cutter is used to cut it out. The cutter consists of a plastic frame with a small blade inside. The blade can be raised or lowered using the orange screw on the top to allow for different thicknesses of paper or photographs. The blade swivels round with the movement of the cutter.

CORNER MOUNTS AND ADHESIVE MOUNTING SQUARES

Corner mounts hold the photo in place yet allow it to be easily removed. They can be plain or have fancy designs. Adhesive mounting squares, which are acid free and sticky on both sides, are applied to the back of the photo. The photo cannot subsequently be removed.

JOURNALING PEN

Any written text should be added to the scrapbook page with a waterproof, fade-proof pigment ink pen. The safest option is to use a journaling pen.

Papers

There is an overwhelming array of papers, stickers and all kinds of other paper embellishments available for use in scrapbooking. Scrapbooking paper may be printed with motifs or designs on such themes such as weddings, christenings or a family tree.

If you want your scrapbooks to last for many generations, you must only use paper that you can be sure is acid free.

Basic Technique PLANNING

Scrapbooking has no boundaries. You can apply most papercrafts to the embellishment of the scrapbook pages, but the photographs should remain the central focus, with the decorative elements complementing the photographs, not competing with them. It is therefore worthwhile spending time planning the look of the pages, and here are some basic dos and don'ts to help you.

DOS

- Be selective with your photographs. Choose and use only the best pictures – those that tell the story or look good together – rather than overcrowding the page.

- Plan a theme or colour scheme for each page to complement or unify the photos.

- Decide on the captions or the text for each page. This will depend on who the scrapbook is aimed at and how long you want it to last. If you are making a family history scrapbook, for instance, you are likely to want more written information to accompany each photograph. On the other hand, if you are making a simple holiday scrapbook, you may only need to include names and dates.

DON'TS

- Don't cut up or crop very old or unique photos. It is easy either to scan the photographs into a computer and output an identical copy or take them to a photographic shop to be copied or for a negative to be produced, from which any number of prints can be made.

- Don't use self-adhesive photo album pages as these will damage your photos.

- Don't place newspaper clippings next to photographs, because newspaper has a very high acid content that will damage the photographs and cause them to deteriorate much more quickly. Photocopy the newspaper onto acid-free paper.

SCRAPBOOK CARE

Avoid cheap scrapbooks – they are unlikely to be acid free. Some scrapbook manufacturers recommend that you store scrapbooks upright so that the weight of the heavily embellished pages does not cause damage to the pages at the back of the scrapbook. All manufacturers agree that scrapbooks must be stored where the temperature does not vary dramatically, so don't store them next to radiators, in attics or in basements.

Further Techniques

CROPPING

With many photos, there is a lot of the image that is neither interesting nor important to its main subject. These photos can be greatly enhanced by homing in on the key interest and trimming off the unimportant surrounding area using a guillotine or scissors. But don't act too hastily – once a photo has been cut, it can't easily be glued back together, and unless you have the negative, it can't be replaced. Stencils can be used to trim photographs into ovals, circles, stars and other fun shapes.

Once a photograph has been trimmed, the corners can be rounded to give a softer effect. A page with many square edges can look harsh, so having some photos with rounded corners will give some visual relief.

COPYING PHOTOS

Many processing shops can now copy photos onto photographic paper while you wait. Use the copies for scrapbooking and store the precious originals.

MOUNTING

Mounting a photograph onto another colour gives it more prominence. This is particularly effective with black and white photographs, where a mount in a soft tone adds a subtle highlight. If you have several photographs on one page, a mount can pick out the central photo and make it the focal point of the page. Coloured mounts should complement the colours in the photograph.

Project

Portrait in Pink Scrapbook Page

Understandably, babies and young children are the most photographed subject of all, resulting in many similar photos being accumulated. Here, five photos were chosen that each told a story but also worked well as a group, sharing the same subject matter and coordinating in colour. By using creative scrapbooking techniques, the photos are cropped, arranged and presented with punched shapes to make a visually exciting scrapbook page.

You will need

several photographs
★
cutting template and cutter
★
scrap paper 30 x 20cm (12 x 8in)
★
cutting mat
★
guillotine and corner rounder
★
scrapbook 29 x 25cm (11½ x 9⅞in)
with plastic inserts
★
pink acid-free paper
28 x 21.5cm (11 x 8½in)
★
adhesive mounting squares
★
border sticker 28cm (11in) long
★
journaling pen (optional)
★
large and small heart punches
★
plain pink and checked pink
acid-free papers 10 x 5cm (4 x 2in)
★
cocktail stick and PVA (white) glue

1 Select five photos to use that combine well visually or tell a story. Using the cutting template and cutter, cut oval, round, heart and square shapes in the piece of scrap paper. Place these cutout shapes over the photos and assess which shape is best for each photo.

2 Place each photo in turn on a cutting mat. Use the cutting template and cutter to cut the photos into your chosen shapes. Here, a guillotine and corner rounder were used to crop three of the photos to rectangular and square shapes.

3 Arrange the five photos on the pink acid-free paper. Move them around until you are happy with the arrangement. Here, the circular photo looked best in the centre of the page. The corners of the two rectangular photos were then trimmed using the circle template and cutter. Use adhesive mounting squares to attach the photos to the pink paper in your chosen arrangement.

5 At this stage, you may decide to write captions or notes to accompany the photos – use a journaling pen for this. Punch large and small heart shapes from the plain pink and pink checked papers. Using a cocktail stick, apply PVA (white) glue to the back of the small hearts and place in a line across the bottom of the page. Glue the large hearts randomly to the pink paper.

4 When all five photos are stuck down, attach a border sticker down the left-hand side of the pink paper, in order to break up the uniform edge of the page.

Even if you are familiar with using cutting templates and a cutter, it is still a good idea to practise on a scrap photo to ensure that you have the blade at the correct height.

Mix & Match

Heart-Felt Greetings

A heart was stamped onto purple card and embossed in gold. It was then cut out and a small piece of blue paper yarn attached to the back with adhesive tape. Purple handmade paper was torn, then stitched with blue paper yarn (see pages 28–31). This was mounted onto a single-fold cream hand-made paper card. The gold-embossed heart was mounted onto a square of the cream handmade paper so that it hangs, 3-D-style, from the paper yarn, then glued to the stitched purple square.

Traveller's Companion

Collage (see pages 26–27) and stamping were combined for this card. Three suitcases descending in size were cut from brown and light brown paper, with tiny luggage labels attached, tied with string – special messages or greetings of your choice could be added to these. Using a felt-tip pen, dashes were marked on the suitcases to represent stitching. The three suitcases were then mounted onto a two-fold cream card using adhesive foam pads. Aeroplanes, cars and trains were stamped over the cream card with blue ink and coloured in with colouring pencils.

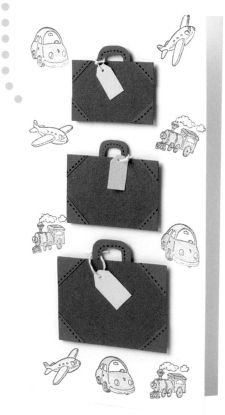

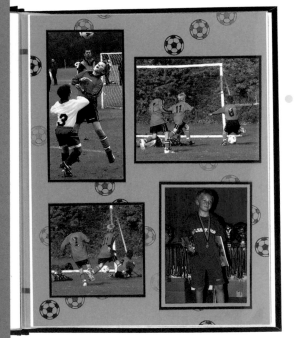

Soccer Success

Soccer is the theme for this scrapbook page. Four chosen photos were cropped with a guillotine, then three were mounted onto black acid-free card. The winning picture was given extra prominence by a double mount of orange and black. Before these were attached to the backing page, a football rubber stamp was inked and then stamped several times over the orange backing page using the fade-out technique on page 97.

Chorus Line
A repeat design need not be repetitive. Here, the same stamp was used to print three girls onto yellow paper, which were then embossed with silver powder. Each girl was coloured in differently using felt-tip pens. The yellow card was cut out and mounted onto a pink single-fold card. Twelve fringed and coiled flowers (see pages 68–69) were made in two shades of pink and glued to the pink card to create a 3-D border. A card featuring two dancing girls would be perfect for twin girls.

Pet-Lover's Delight
This ultra-speedy card design, which can be made in less than 30 minutes, features a playful kitten stamped on cream card and coloured in with watercolour pencils, the colours blended with a damp paintbrush. It was then cut out and mounted onto an orange single-fold card. Single strands from a length of string were used to make two balls of string, then glued to the card with lively trailing ends

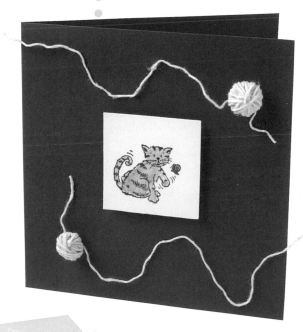

Silver-Leaf Gift Box
A gift box was made from mauve card using the template on page 126 and following the technique on page 18. Before it was assembled, leaves were stamped and embossed in silver around the four edges. Two leaf shapes were stamped and embossed in silver on the lid of the box. Working from the underside of the lid, two leaf shapes were pricked (see pages 86–87). The box was then assembled. Elements of the design could be used to create a matching greetings card, and a silver-embossed leaf would make an attractive coordinating gift tag.

Three-Dimensional & Motion

PAPER SCULPTURE • PAPER ARCHITECTURE • POP-UP

These simple yet sophisticated papercrafts set out to defy one of paper's defining characteristics, its flatness. In paper sculpture, paper is subtly modelled and shaped to exploit the natural action of light and shadow, whereas more structured forms are created with paper architecture by making carefully placed cuts and folds.

Pop-up techniques use movement to animate greetings cards ingeniously, giving them an added dimension of surprise. Crafters of every ability and experience will enjoy exploring the essential qualities of paper in paper sculpture — its weight, grain and texture — and how to use these to maximum effect. Pop-up also offers something for everyone, with its fun element and ability to engage the recipient in an interactive response. In Mix & Match, companion papercrafts are also brought into play, complementing the impressive display of 3-D and motion features.

Clockwise from left: Halloween Spooks Card, pages 120–121; Lotus Flower Gift Box, page 115; Glittering Hearts Card, page 117; Pink Elephant Card, pages 122–123; Crowning Glory, page 124

Paper Sculpture

This term sounds very grand and artistic but it is simply the craft of curling, scoring and folding paper. By expanding on techniques already known to many crafters, a sheet of flat paper is transformed from the two-dimensional to the three-dimensional. Paper sculpture is a subtle, delicate art and therefore not suitable for making items to be sent through the mail, where they would be crushed.

Paper sculpture requires an understanding of paper and its properties but no specific tools as such. Sensational results can therefore be achieved with just a little know-how and practice.

Basic Tool Kit

SCORING TOOL
An empty ballpoint pen is used for scoring paper. The pointed edge of a bone folder can also be used to score paper.

CURLING TOOLS
Anything object that is round and smooth can be used for curling paper, the diameter of which will determine the degree of curl. Appropriate items include a cocktail stick, paintbrush and a length of wooden dowel.

Papers

White paper is popular for paper sculpture because it accentuates the shadows created. However, paper of any colour or texture can be used. Avoid heavy papers as they are not easily curled and some papers are resistant to curling because of the grain of the paper (see Basic Technique below).

Basic Technique

In paper sculpture, the shape is cut out first and then it is curled, scored or folded. The basic techniques for scoring and folding are demonstrated on page 12.

CURLING
Not all papers liked to be curled and this is where the grain of the paper comes into play. Find the grain of your paper by rolling it one way and then the other way – the easiest will indicate the direction of the grain, and this is the direction in which you need to curl.

FORMING FINE OR SMALL COILS
If you want to make a fine coil with a narrow strip of paper, you could use a quilling tool – see page 64.

1 Take your paper and roll it tightly around a length of wooden dowel.

2 Let go of the paper, remove the dowel and see how it springs back yet the curl remains. You can see here how loose the curl is compared to that made by rolling paper around a paintbrush and a cocktail stick – the smaller the item used to curl around, the tighter the curl.

Project Lotus Flower Gift Box

Simple flower shapes are brought to life with the three-dimensional element of paper sculpture and used to transform a plain, silver gift box.

You will need

pencil

★

scrap card

★

scissors

★

light blue, mid blue and dark blue
paper each 15 x 10cm (6 x 4in)

★

fine paintbrush

★

PVA (white) glue

★

cocktail stick

★

regular hole punch

★

silver card 25 x 45cm (9⅞ x 17¾in)

1 Make a gift box from silver card using the template on page 126 and following the instructions on page 18. Make your own card template from the flower template on page 130 (see Step 1, page 16). Use the template to cut four flowers from light blue, four from mid blue and one from dark blue paper with scissors. Take one flower and roll each petal around the rounded end of a fine paintbrush to curl. Repeat with the remaining flowers.

2 Take a curled flower and, using your fingers, push the petals together. They will spring back a little but this gives the flower more shape. Repeat with the remaining curled flowers.

If you don't feel confident enough to position the flowers on the box by eye, mark where they are to be glued with small pencil marks — PVA (white) glue dries quickly and you won't be able to rearrange the flowers once it has dried.

3 Using PVA (white) glue applied with a cocktail stick, glue the dark blue flower to the centre of the box. Glue the mid blue and light blue flowers around this to form a square. Using the hole punch, punch eight circles from the silver card. Glue a circle to the centre of each flower.

Paper Architecture

This is a technique where precise cuts and folds in a single sheet of paper create a three-dimensional design. Paper architecture is a form of pop-up as the design springs up when the card is opened. But whereas pop-up uses separate pieces of paper, paper architecture's three-dimensional effects are achieved with just one piece of paper. Paper architecture became popular in the 1980s with the work of Masahiro Chatani. His extremely intricate designs of castles and other beautiful buildings are quite amazing. Chatani used only white paper, relying on shadows to highlight his designs. However, paper architecture doesn't have to be overly complicated, as simple designs can look equally stunning.

Basic Tool Kit

CRAFT KNIFE AND SCORING TOOL

A sharp craft knife is needed for making neat, precise cuts, and you will need an empty ballpoint pen for scoring.

CUTTING MAT AND METAL RULER

It is essential to work on a self-healing cutting mat and to make cuts against a metal ruler – the blade of the craft knife can easily damage a plastic ruler.

Papers

Medium-weight paper is required or the design will be too heavy for the paper to support. Paper with an interesting texture or a printed design can add an extra dimension to this craft.

Basic Technique

For paper architecture to work well, clean, precise cuts need to be executed, combined with neat scoring and folding. The following steps demonstrate the making of a simple shape, but the basic principles are the same for all kinds of structures.

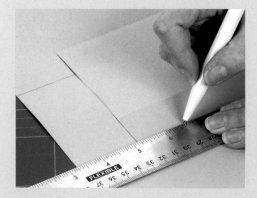

1 Cut two vertical parallel lines 15cm (6in) long and 10cm (4in) apart in the centre of a sheet of paper. Measure a horizontal line 3cm (1⅛in) up from the base of the two cuts. Score along this line between the two cuts using a scoring tool against a metal ruler. Turn the paper over. Measure a line 3cm (1⅛in) below the top of the two cuts. Score along this line either side of the two cuts to the edges of the paper, then score between the two cuts at the top and the bottom. This leaves three score lines on the rectangle and two score lines either side of the rectangle.

2 Place your fingers on the score lines either side of the rectangle. Gently fold the top of the paper towards you and the rectangle will start to emerge from the paper towards you. Continue folding the paper over and press down to make the folds along the score lines.

Glittering Hearts Card

This impressive greetings card uses the principles of paper architecture to make a pyramid of hearts protrude from the front of the card.

You will need

pencil
★
metal ruler
★
red card 30 x 12cm (12 x 4¾in)
★
tracing paper
★
cutting mat
★
craft knife
★
scoring tool
★
glitter glue

Glitter glue takes a long time to dry, so leave it overnight to dry thoroughly.

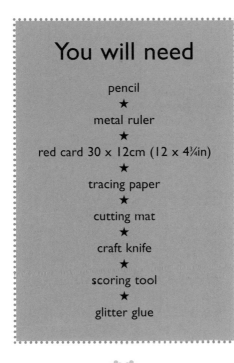

1 Using a pencil, draw a horizontal line 3.5cm (1⅜in) from the base of the red card. Trace the heart template from page 132 centrally onto the right side of the red card, lining up the bottom three hearts with the pencil line. Place the red card on a cutting mat and carefully cut along the solid lines with a craft knife.

2 Using the scoring tool against a metal ruler, score along the lower dashed score lines marked on the design either side of the heart pyramid to the outside edges of the card. Turn the card over to the wrong side and score along the continuous dashed score line right across the card.

3 Fold along the score lines so that the score is inside the fold in each case – the heart pyramid will then stand out. Use glitter glue to outline all the hearts in the pyramid.

Pop-Up

This is a term used for three-dimensional paper structures that spring up when a card or book is opened. In pop-up, many different pieces of paper can be cut, folded and glued together to form the design, rather than using a single sheet of paper as in paper architecture. 'Pop-up' now covers other interactive elements such as flaps and pull-outs, although this is sometimes referred to as paper engineering.

The first pop-up books were published around 1855 and were designed to amuse children. Now, pop-up books and greetings cards are a huge industry. Pop-up is popular with children and adults alike because we all love the element of surprise and humour. It relies on accurate measuring and scoring, but once this basic skill is mastered, it is easy to make spectacular cards.

Basic Tool Kit

CUTTING MAT
It is essential to work on a self-healing cutting mat.

CRAFT KNIFE
A sharp craft knife is needed for cutting out pop-up motifs.

SET SQUARE
This is an important tool for pop-up, since angles and lines need to be accurate for cutting, otherwise the design won't work.

METAL RULER
Cutting with a craft knife must be done against a metal ruler – the craft knife can easily damage a plastic ruler.

SCORING TOOL
You will need an empty ballpoint pen for scoring tabs on the motifs on which they fold down and pop up.

GLUE STICK
This is ideal for applying glue to the scored tabs on the pop-up motifs to attach them to the card base.

Papers

If the paper used is too thin, the pop-up will not stand up, but if the paper is too thick, it will not fold. As a general guide, paper between 135 and 200gsm is recommended, that is from medium-weight to relatively heavyweight. Ordinary machine-made papers are best for pop-up but these can be embellished with other decorative papers (see Butterfly Hover in the Mix & Match section on page 124).

Basic Techniques

PULL-OUTS

The movement of pull-outs is dependent on somebody pulling! Pull-outs add an element of surprise and fun. Many card makers overlook this simple technique, but it should be in everyone's papercraft repertoire.

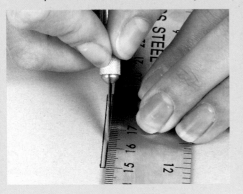

1 Using a craft knife and ruler, cut two vertical parallel lines of equal length 2mm (³⁄₂in) apart in a piece of card. Remove the strip by cutting horizontally between the lines. This creates a slot for the pull-tab. If only one cut is made, the hole will not be wide enough for the pull-tab to pass through.

2 Cut another piece of card into a 'T' shape. This is called the pull-tab. The width of this pull-tab needs to be 4mm (⅛in) shorter than the slot and the top of the 'T' shape needs to be 2cm (¾in) wider than the slot. This cross piece stops the pull-tab from being pulled all the way out of the slot. Turn the card right-side down and insert the pull-tab into the slot.

3 Glue a strip of paper either side of the pull-tab 3cm (1⅛in) from the slot. This strip holds the pull-tab in place as it is pulled in and out. Turn the card over and add a picture or message of your choice to the pull-out.

V FOLD

There are many techniques used in pop-up but this next basic one provides the foundation for more sophisticated designs. The V fold is so called simply because it forms a 'V' shape. 'The base' refers to the single-fold card to which the V fold is glued and the 'glue tabs' are flaps that are glued onto the base.

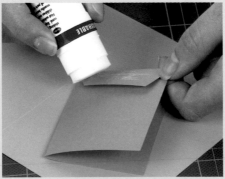

1 Fold a rectangle of paper in half. Make two glue tabs by scoring across the base of the rectangle, then fold the tabs at right angles. Using a glue stick, apply glue to the underside of the glue tab and stick it down onto the base at a 45-degree angle to the centre fold. Make sure that the crease of the folded paper is in line with the centre fold on the base.

2 Apply glue to the other glue tab in the same way.

3 Fold the base over onto the glued tab. Press down to ensure that the glue tab has found its correct position.

4 When the glue has dried, open up the base and the paper will pop up.

Project Halloween Spooks Card

This Halloween concertina card is full of creepy crawlies and the ghost on the pull-out makes a spooky surprise appearance!

You will need

scoring tool
★
metal ruler
★
2 pieces of orange card
21.5 x 30cm (8½ x 12in) and
5.5 x 1cm (2¼ x ⅜in)
★
pencil and scrap card
★
scissors
★
white pencil
★
black paper
21 x 30cm (8¼ x 12in)
★
black card
14 x 7cm (5½ x 2¾in)
★
cutting mat and craft knife
★
glue stick
★
white card
5 x 10cm (2 x 4in)
★
black pen
★
white tissue paper
20 x 30cm (8 x 12in)
★
small scissors
★
six wiggly eyes
★
superglue

1 Using the scoring tool against a metal ruler, score two vertical lines on the rectangle of orange card at 6cm (2⅜in) and 18cm (7in) from the left-hand short edge. Turn the card over and score two more lines at 12cm (4¾in) and 24cm (9½in) from the right-hand edge. Fold the card along each score line with the score inside the fold, to make a concertina.

2 Make your own card templates using the spider and bat templates on page 132 (see Step 1, page 16). Using a white pencil, draw round these templates onto black paper to make three spiders and four bats and cut out with scissors.

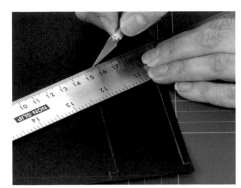

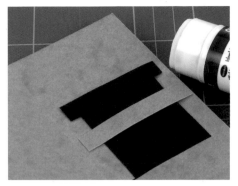

3 In the same way, make your own card template from the 'T'-shape template on page 132 for the pull-tab. Using a white pencil, draw round the template onto black card. Cut out using a craft knife against a metal ruler on a cutting mat.

4 Place the orange card right-side up on the cutting mat. Using a craft knife, cut a horizontal slot centrally in the left hand panel 10cm (4in) from the top edge 4.5cm (1¾in) long and 2mm (³⁄₃₂in) wide.

5 Turn the orange card over and insert the pull-tab in the slot. Using a glue stick, glue the strip of orange card over the pull-tab 3cm (1⅛in) above the slot.

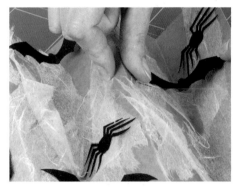

6 In the same way as before, use the template on page 132 to cut a ghost shape from white card. Using a black pen, draw on the eyes and a mouth. Glue the ghost to the front of the pull-tab.

7 Tear the white tissue paper into irregular pieces. Using the glue stick, glue the tissue paper pieces randomly to the orange card. Glue a spider above the pull-out ghost and two more to the inside of the folds. Using one hand, pick up a wiggly eye between the points of a small pair of scissors and, with the other hand, dab a dot of superglue onto the back of the wiggly eye. Attach to a spider. Glue two wiggly eyes to each spider.

8 Take one of the bat shapes and fold in half. Using the glue stick, apply glue to the tip of each wing and position across an inside fold of the card – the wing tips must be near outside folds. Glue the other three bats to the card in the same way.

More pull-outs could be added to this card with scary images or Halloween messages written on them.

Project Pink Elephant Card

Who can resist a bright pink mother and baby elephant? Children and grown-ups alike are sure to adore this jolly jungle card.

You will need

handmade paper in three shades
of green 15 x 10cm (6 x 4in)
★
glue stick
★
single-fold green card
12 x 24cm (4¾ x 9½in)
★
scrap card
★
pencil
★
scissors
★
pink card 12 x 20cm
(4¾ x 8in)
★
cutting mat
★
cutting knife
★
scoring tool
★
metal ruler
★
white paper 4cm (1½in) square
★
black pen

1 Tear the green handmade paper into strips. Using a glue stick, glue the strips to the inside of the green single-fold card, covering the entire card. This will form the base of the card.

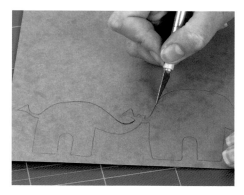

2 Make your own card template from the elephant template on page 133 (see Step 1, page 16). Using a pencil, draw round the template onto pink card. Place the pink card on the cutting mat. Using a craft knife, cut round the outline of the elephants.

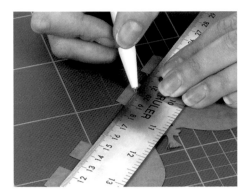

3 Using the scoring tool against a metal ruler, score along the four dashed glue tab lines as marked on the template.

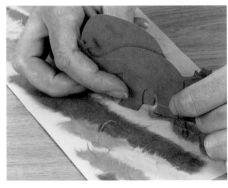

4 Using a glue stick, apply glue to the undersides of the two glue tabs of the small elephant. Place it on the left-hand side of the base at a 45-degree angle to the centre fold – the point at which the trunk of the small elephant meets the tail of the large elephant should be aligned with the centre fold of the base card.

5 Apply glue to the undersides of the two glue tabs of the larger elephant.

6 Fold the base card over onto these glue tabs and press down firmly so that the glue tabs are stuck in place on the base. Leave to dry.

7 Using the templates on page 133, cut one large and one small ear from pink card. Score along the dashed glue tab lines as marked on the template. Apply glue to the undersides of the two glue tabs and attach to the elephants. Using the templates on page 133, cut one small and one large tusk from white paper and glue to each elephant. Use a black pen to mark an eye on each elephant.

You can adapt this project to create alternative designs by using different jungle animals, such as hippos, zebras or giraffes.

Mix & Match

Surprise Gifts

Squares of green giftwrap were folded using the tea bag folding technique on page 51. The squares were of decreasing sizes so when attached to the red card formed a tree shape. A slot was cut in the red card and a pull-tab made. An image of presents was stamped onto the pull-tab (see pages 96–97) and coloured in using felt-tip pens (see page 100). Snowflakes were then stamped over the card. A personal message could be added to the pull-tab.

Crowning Glory

A crown was cut from a piece of silver card, using the paper architecture technique on page 116, and the base embossed with dots using a fine ball embossing tool (see page 77). The circles were punched using a hole punch and glued to the crown. Glitter glue gives the three points of the crown a sparkle. A spiral hole punch was used to punch spirals from red giftwrap (see page 22) and these decorate the background of the card. This design could be adapted to feature a tiara for a little girl.

Butterfly Hover

A butterfly was made from pink paper and decorated with holographic paper. It was then attached to a single-fold yellow card using the V-fold technique on page 119. Two smaller butterflies and leaves decorate the card. You could adapt the design to create a single pop-up butterfly resting on a flower, or make an arrangement of pop-up flowers for a Mother's Day card.

Fly Me to the Moon

A space rocket shape was cut from silver card and attached to a single-fold blue card using adhesive foam pads. A fine ball embossing tool was used to emboss dots in the silver portholes and strips for a studded effect (see pages 88–91). Torn pieces of orange and yellow paper were attached to the bottom for fire. A picture of the earth was cut from a magazine and attached to the card. Tiny dots of glitter glue give the effect of stars.

Enscrolled Gift Bag

This gift bag was made from pink handmade paper using an empty box as a mould (see page 17). A strip of parchment paper was sewn to the bag for a handle using embroidery thread (see pages 28–31). Strips of parchment paper were curled around a paintbrush and attached to the bag. A scroll was glued to the sides of the bag for a finishing decorative touch.

Festive Tags

Holly-shaped leaves were cut from green paper, then scored down the centre and at angles to give the impression of veins. The leaves were gently pushed into shape and glued to green gift tags. Strips of red 3mm (⅛in) wide quilling paper were made into tight coils (see pages 64–65) to resemble berries and glued to the tags. Mistletoe tags could be made in the same way.

Templates

GIFT BOX
PAGE 18
ENLARGE BY 50%

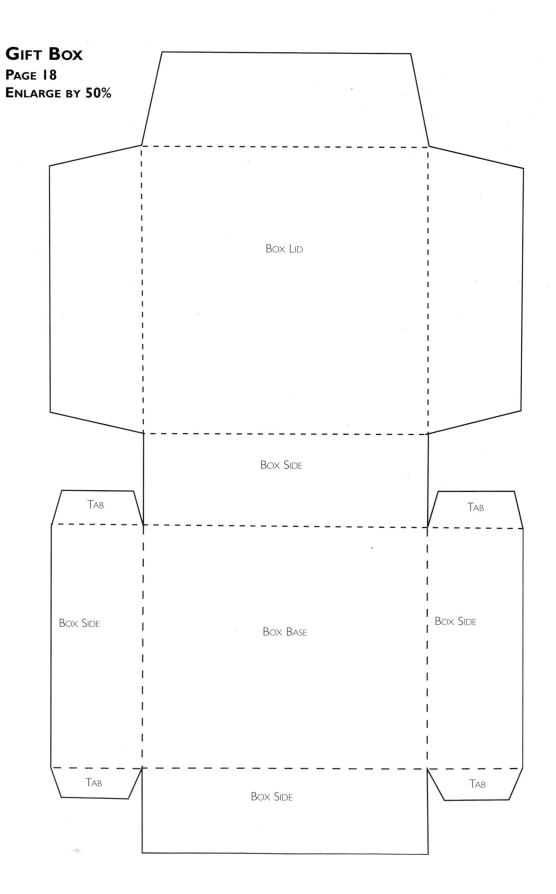

BOX LID

BOX SIDE

TAB

TAB

BOX SIDE

BOX BASE

BOX SIDE

TAB

TAB

BOX SIDE

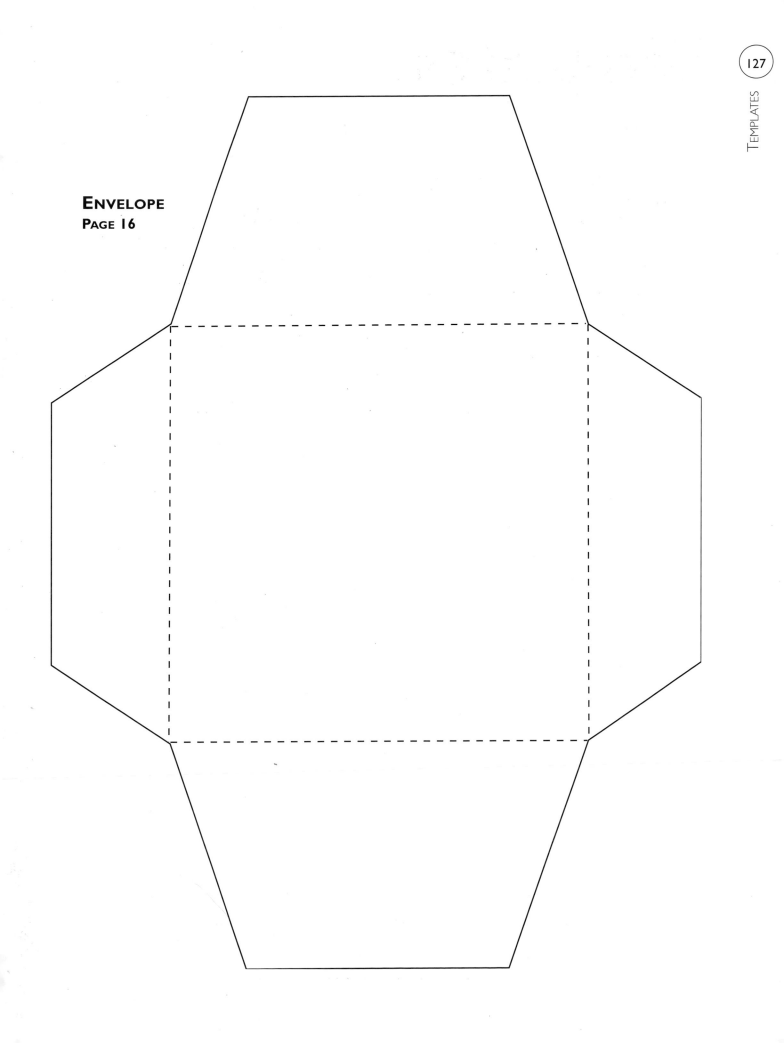

ENVELOPE
PAGE 16

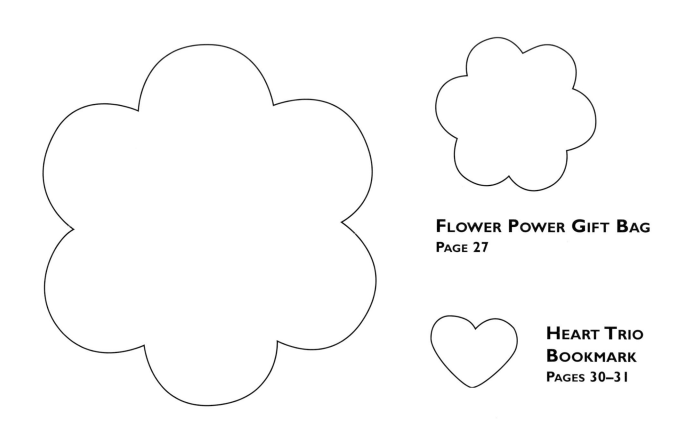

FLOWER POWER GIFT BAG
PAGE 27

HEART TRIO
BOOKMARK
PAGES 30–31

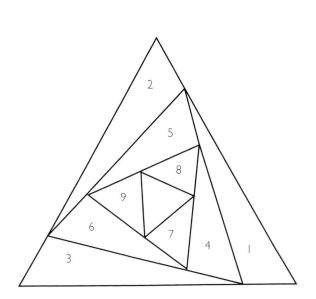

IRIS FOLDING TEMPLATE
PAGE 55

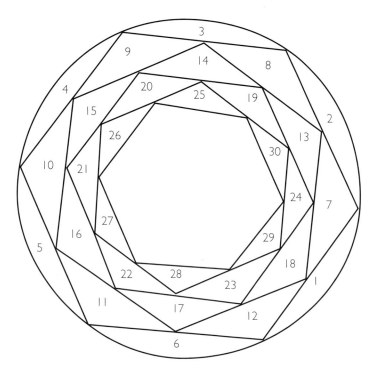

BLAZING SUN CARD
PAGES 56–57

ROSETTE HAT CARD
PAGES 52–53

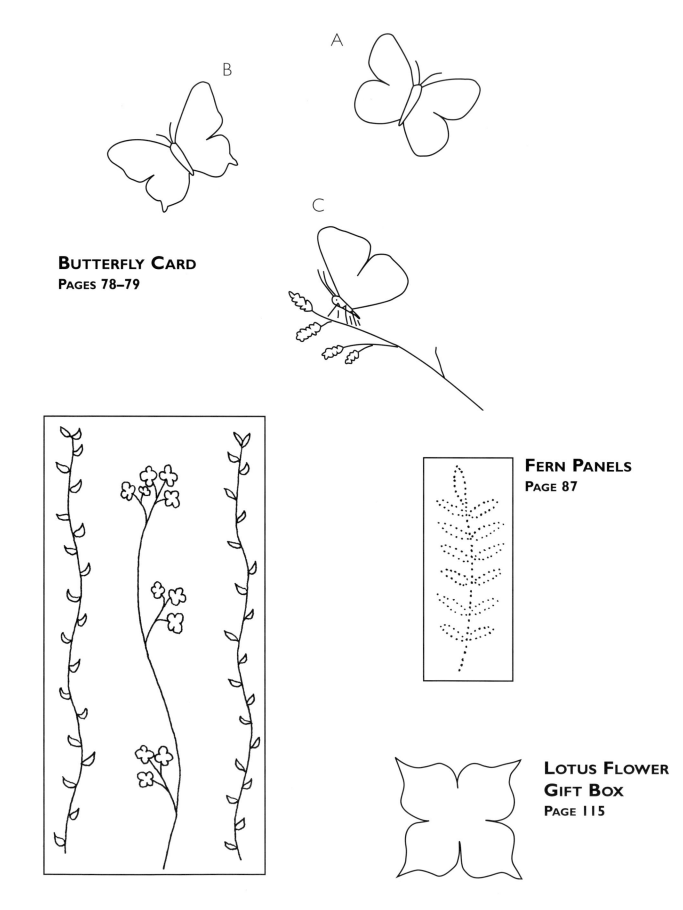

B

A

C

BUTTERFLY CARD
PAGES 78–79

FERN PANELS
PAGE 87

LOTUS FLOWER
GIFT BOX
PAGE 115

FLORAL GARLAND CARD
PAGES 84–85

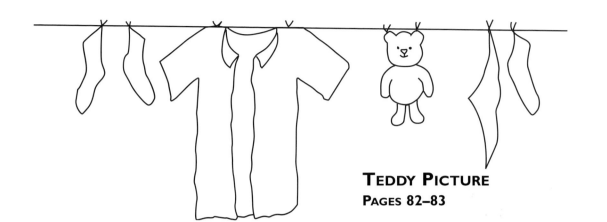

TEDDY PICTURE
PAGES 82–83

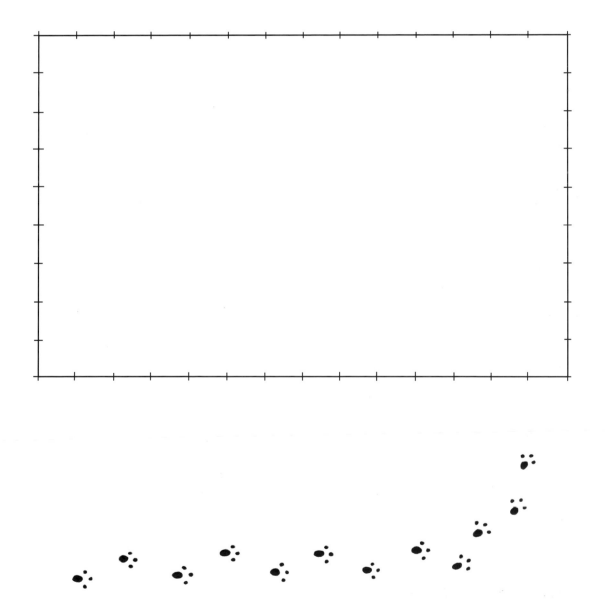

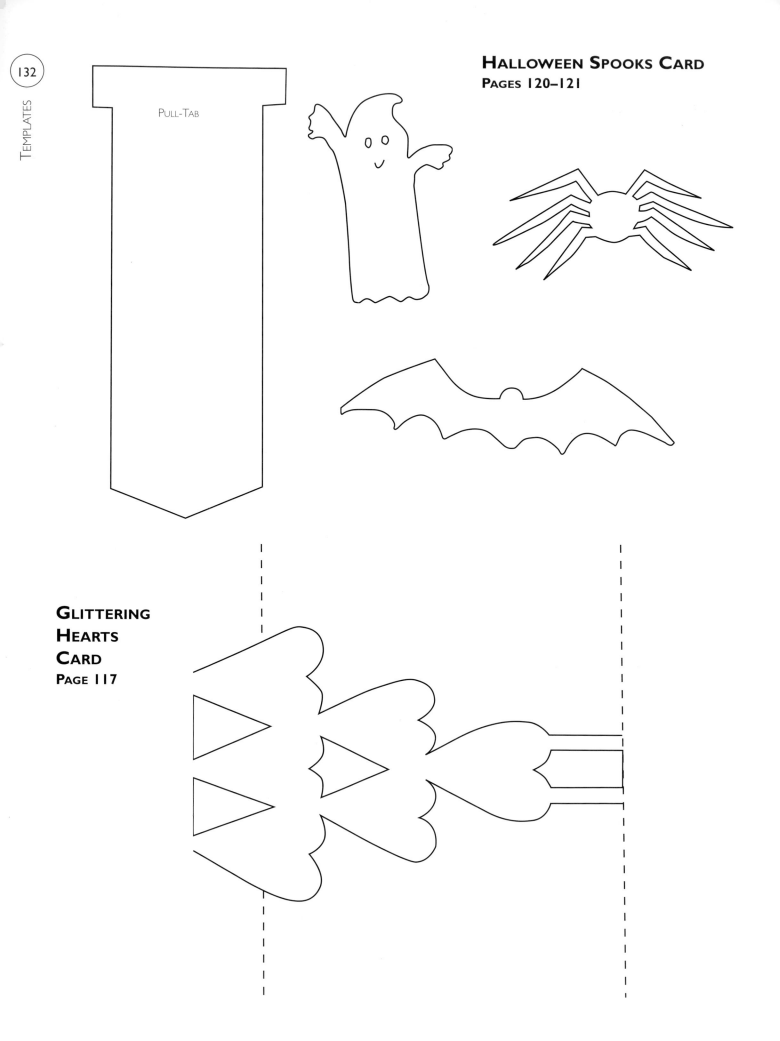

PULL-TAB

HALLOWEEN SPOOKS CARD
PAGES 120–121

**GLITTERING
HEARTS
CARD**
PAGE 117

PINK ELEPHANT CARD
PAGES 122–123

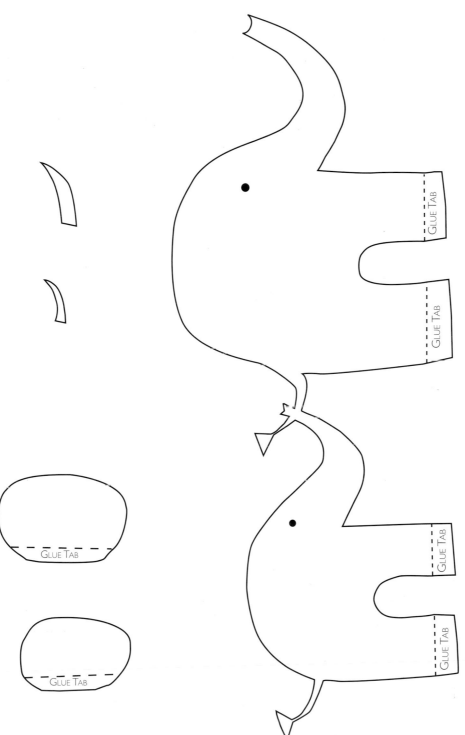

GLUE TAB

GLUE TAB

GLUE TAB

GLUE TAB

GLUE TAB

GLUE TAB

Suppliers

UK

THE ART OF CRAFT LTD
248 Shawfield Road
Ash
Aldershot GU12 5DJ
tel: 01252 334855
fax: 01252 314558
email: jane@crochet-too.demon.co.uk
www.crochet-too.demon.co.uk
General papercraft retailer including punches, pricking and embossing templates, Lacé® tools and equipment.

CASPARI LTD
9 Shire Hill
Saffron Walden
Essex CB11 3AP
tel: 01799 51301
email: caspari@hgcaspari.com
www.casparius.com
Paper napkin and handkerchief manufacturers. Contact for local retailers.

CENTAGRAPH
18 Station Parade
Harrogate
North Yorkshire HG1 1UE
tel: 01423 566327
fax: 01423 505486
email: info@centagraph.co.uk
www.centagraph.co.uk
General papercraft retailer including punches, tea bag folding papers and mizuhiki cords.

CRAFT CREATIONS LTD
Ingersoll House
Delamare Road
Cheshunt
Hertfordshire EN8 9HD
tel: 01992 781900
fax: 01992 634339
email: enquiries@craftcreations.com
www.craftcreations.co.uk
Greetings card blanks and general craft retailer. Mail order or contact for local stockist.

CRAFTWORK CARDS
Unit 7
The Moorings
Waterside Road
Stourton
Leeds
West Yorkshire LS10 1DG
tel: 0113 276 5713
fax: 0113 270 5986
email: sue@craftworkcards.freeserve.co.uk
www.craftworkcards.com
Greetings card blanks, paper and card retailer.

DESIGN OBJECTIVES LTD
36–44 Willis Way
Fleet Industrial Estate
Poole
Dorset BH15 3SU
tel: 01202 679976
email: info@designobjectives.com
www.docrafts.co.uk
Distributor of Anita's Art and Whispers rubber stamps and many other craft products. Contact for local stockist.

HOBBYCRAFT STORES
tel: 0800 027 2387 for nearest store or mail order is available.
www.hobbycraft.co.uk
General craft retailer of a wide range of papercraft supplies including rubber stamps.

HOMECRAFTS DIRECT
PO Box 38
Leicester LE1 9BU
tel: 0845 458 4531
email: info@homecrafts.co.uk
www.homecrafts.co.uk
General craft supplies including craft kits and books. Mail order.

GLENNIS GILRUTH
17 High Street
Great Houghton
Barnsley S72 0AA
tel: 01709 897416
email: paperdeluxe@hotmail.com
Paper yarn supplier. Mail order.

IMPRESS CARDS AND CRAFT MATERIALS
Slough Farm
Westhall
Halesworth
Suffolk IP19 8RN
tel: 01986 781 422
fax: 01986 781 677
email: enquiries@impresscards.com
www.impresscards.com
Greetings card blanks and craft supplies. Mail order or call for local stockist.

JANE JENKINS QUILLING DESIGN
33 Mill Rise
Skidby
Cottingham
East Yorkshire HU16 5UA
tel: 01482 843721
fax: 01482 840783
email: enquiries@jjquilling.co.uk
www.jjquilling.co.uk
Quilling papers, tools and equipment. Mail order.

LJ GIBBS & PARTNERS LTD
Mulberry House
Hewitts Road
Orpington
Kent BR6 7QS
tel: 01959 533 663
fax: 01959 534 082
email: info@ljgibbsandpartners.com
www.ljgibbsandpartners.com
Handmade paper supplier.

MAMELOK PRESS
Northern Way
Bury St Edmunds
Suffolk IP32 6NJ
tel: 01284 762291
fax: 01284 703689
email: chris@mamelok.com
www.mamelok.co.uk
Découpage printed paper supplier. Mail order.

THE SCRAPBOOK HOUSE
Unit 9, Cromwell Business Park
Banbury Road
Chipping Norton
Oxford OX7 5SR
tel: 0870 770 7717
fax: 01608 643 430
email: sales@thescrapbookhouse.com
www.thescrapbookhouse.com
*Scrapbook papers, tools and equipment
including rubber stamps.*

WENDY'S ART WORKS
Keepers Cottage
Deene Road
Harringworth
Corby NN17 3AB
tel: 01780 450616
fax: 01780 450267
email: info@wendysartworks.com
www.wendysartworks.com
*Blank wooden boxes and découpage
papers. Mail order.*

EUROPE
IDEAL HOME RANGE
email: info@ihr-online.de
www.idealhomerange.com
*Paper napkin manufacturer. Contact for
local stockists.*

KARS CREATIVE WHOLESALE
Industrieweg 27
Industrieterrein 'De Heuning'
Postbus 97
4050 EB Ochten
The Netherlands
tel: +31(0) 344 642864
fax: +31(0) 344 643509
email: info@kars.nl
www.kars.nl
*Contact for local stockists of Pergamano®,
Lacé® and Fiskars® products.*

PERGAMANO® INTERNATIONAL
Po Box 86
1420 AB Uithoorn
The Netherlands
fax: +31(0)297 526256
www.pergamano.com
*Parchment craft manufacturers. Contact for
local stockist.*

USA
AMERICAN TRADITIONAL DESIGNS
442 First NH Turnpike
Northwood
NH 03261
tel: 800 448 6656
fax: 800 448 6654
email: office@americantraditional.com
www.americantraditional.com
*Embossing stencils manufacturers. Contact
for local stockists.*

CREATIVE MEMORIES®
3001 Clearwater Road
PO Box 1839
St Cloud MN 56302-1839
email: US@creative-memories.com
www.creativememories.com
*Scrapbooking suppliers. Contact to locate
nearest Creative Memories® consultant.*

CREATIVE PAPERS ONLINE
HANDMADE PAPER
PO Box 133
Pinckney
Michigan 48169
tel: 734 878 4895
fax: 734 878 1738
email: sales@handmade-paper.us
www.handmade-paper.us
Handmade paper supplier.

HOT OFF THE PRESS INC (includes
Paper Pizazz™ and Paper Flair™)
1250 NW Third
Canby OR 97013
tel: 800 227 9595
fax: 503 266 8749
email: info@hotp.com
www.craftpizazz.com
*Printed papers. Mail order or contact for
local stockist.*

MICHAELS' STORES
8000 Bent Branch Dr
Irving TX 75063
tel: 800 642 4235
www.michaels.com
*General craft suppliers including handmade
paper and scrapbooking.*

STAMPORIUM
10116 - 50th Pl.w.
Mukilteo
Washington WE 98275
tel: 425 348 7400
fax: 425 348 0818
email: tj@stamporium.com
www.stamporium.com
Papercraft supplier, including Lacé®.

AUSTRALIA
PARCHMENT CRAFT AUSTRALIA
PO Box 1026 Elizabeth Vale
South Australia 5112
email: sales@parchcraftaustralia.com
www.parchcraftaustralia.com
Wholesaler of parchment craft products.

Craft Guilds
QUILLING GUILD
The Guild, formed in 1983, aims to
promote the art of quilling and the
knowledge of quill work. Although based
in the UK, it publishes a newsletter three
times a year called *Quillers Today* with
useful information and quilling designs,
which is available worldwide. You don't
have to be an expert in quilling to join
the Quilling Guild.
email: quillguild@aol.com
www.quilling-guild.co.uk

NATIONAL GUILD OF
DÉCOUPEURS
Founded in 1971, this non-profit
organization is dedicated to providing
education in the art of découpage, to
encouraging a high level of quality and to
offering an exchange of creative ideas.
www.decoupage.org

DÉCOUPAGE GUILD AUSTRALIA INC
In 1984 the Découpage Guild Australia
(a non-profit organization) was formed in
Melbourne by a group of ten découpage
enthusiasts. Découpage Guild Australia Inc.
has members throughout the country.
email: info@decoupage.com.au
www.decoupage.com.au

Glossary

The definitions given in this glossary are in the context of papercrafts.

aperture
a hole cut into paper or card which may be square, rectangular, circular or otherwise shaped.

appliqué
paper laid onto another layer of paper and held in place by glue or stitching.

collage
an arrangement of papers, or various materials, glued together to form a design.

concertina
alternate folding of paper or card so that it expands and contracts.

crimper
an alternative name for a ribbler.

découpage
the practice of cutting out paper images, gluing them to an object, then covering with coats of varnish.

duo card
a sheet of card that has a different colour either side.

embossing
to raise an image in relief.

embossing in parchment craft
where pressure is applied to parchment paper using embossing tools.

embossing in rubber stamping
the technique of applying special embossing powder to a design and then heating it so that it melts to become raised and shiny.

fringing
cutting a piece of paper into strips where the cut strips are held by an uncut margin at the top of the paper.

grain
the direction in which the fibres of paper lie.

handmade paper
paper without a grain, so that the fibres lie randomly.

inkpad
the foam layer in which ink is stored for rubber stamping.

iris folding
the layering of folded papers to resemble the iris of an eye or a camera.

Lacé®
the technique of cutting, scoring, folding and tucking paper using a metal template.

mizuhiki
the art of ceremonial Japanese cord tying. The name is now given to the craft of creating motifs and pictures with mizuhiki cords.

mizuhiki cords
lengths of twisted paper covered with metallic paper.

napkin découpage
where the images from paper napkins are cut out and used for découpage.

paper architecture
the craft of cutting, scoring and folding paper to create a three-dimensional pop-up design.

paper sculpture
the craft of making paper three-dimensional by curling, scoring and folding.

parchment craft
where parchment paper is embossed to create a raised image.

parchment paper
translucent paper used in parchment craft.

ply
a layer of fine paper; a paper napkin may be referred to as three-ply, made up of three fine layers.

pop-up
paper that rises or moves when a card or book is opened. Pop-up also covers pull-tabs and slide movements that require interaction.

pricking
piercing holes in paper using a needle to create a design.

punches
metal cutters into which paper is placed, then when pressure is applied to the cutter, the shape is punched out.

quilling
rolling narrow strips of paper to form designs; sometimes referred to as paper filigree.

ribbler
two patterned cogs into which paper is fed; the turning of the cogs impresses the pattern onto the paper.

rubber stamp
a design cut into a rubber pad which is mounted onto wood or foam.

rubber stamping
the technique of printing using a rubber stamp and inkpad.

score
a linear indent made on paper or card in order to make a fold in the paper.

scrapbooking
the name given to the craft of arranging, mounting and embellishing photos in a scrapbook (album).

stamping
an abbreviation of rubber stamping.

tea bag folding
the craft of folding squares of paper and arranging in a rosette shape.

vellum
translucent paper with a printed pattern.

weave
strips of paper interlaced to form a single piece of paper.

Acknowledgments

Many thanks to Fiona Eaton, Lisa Forrester, Ali Myer and Jennifer Proverbs of David & Charles.

Special thanks to Jo Richardson, Karl Adamson and Stewart Mills.

About the author

Elizabeth Moad has practised crafts for several years, attending craft fairs and contributing to crafts magazines. Her passion for papercrafts led her to undertake further study in order to pursue a creative career. This is her first book for David & Charles. Elizabeth lives in Norwich, East Anglia, in the UK.

Index

apertures, cutting and mounting 14–15; iris folding 40, 54–7
appliqué 20, 28–31

bags 17, 20, 27, 72–3, 90, 92, 125, 128
basic papercrafting techniques 12–15
bookmarks 24, 30–1, 49, 93, 128
borders, embossed 83; pricked 38, 86; punched 22, 24; stickers 109; woven 42
boxes 18, 20, 34–5, 61, 92, 111, 115, 126

cards, cutting, scoring and folding 11–12; pre-cut 11
clubs 11
coiling 65–7, 72–3, 111, 114, 125
collage 20, 26–7, 38, 39, 61, 110
colour, colouring papers 26; duo-coloured card 44–9, 61; overlaying 26; parchment craft 81–5; rubber stamping 100–3, 104, 110–11, 124; weaving 42
concertina folding 72
copyright 11
corner mounts 106
corners, corner punch 22, 24; corner rounder 106
corrugated papers 6, 27
crimping see ribbling
cropping 107
curling 114–15, 125
cut out techniques 20–39
cutting 13, 80
    apertures 14

découpage 20, 32–7, 39; paper napkin découpage 20, 36–7, 38
double-sided adhesive tape 8, 15
dual-tip pens and dabbers 96
duo-coloured card 44–9, 61

edges, cutting 13; fancy-edged scissors 9, 73, 92; torn 12–13
embossed papers 6
embossing, paper 39, 81–5, 88–91 93, 125; parchment paper 74, 76–9, 92; rubber stamping 73, 104–5, 110–11, 124
embroidered papers 6
embroidery 20, 28–31, 38–9, 72, 110
envelopes 16, 60, 91, 93, 98–9, 127
eyes, wiggly 67, 120–1

festive 42, 124, 125
filigree see quilling
foam pads, adhesive 8, 15, 102–3
folding 12, 45; concertina 72; iris 40, 54–7, 128; Lacé® 40, 44–9, 60, 61; tea bag 40, 50–3, 60, 61, 73, 124
frames 39, 70–1
fringing 62, 64, 68–71, 72, 111

gift bags see bags
gift boxes see boxes
gift tags see tags
giftwrap 105
glues 8; glitter glues 8, 117, 124, 125; superglue 67
guilds 11

holographic paper 54, 56–7, 124

inserts, mounting 14–15
iris folding 40, 54–7, 128

kaleidoscope folding see tea bag folding
knots 58–9

Lacé® 40, 44–9, 60, 61
lighting 10

masking 101, 102–3
metallic embossing powders 104–5
metallic papers 61
mizuhiki 37, 40, 58–9, 60, 73
mounting, apertures 14–15; parchment paper 79, 85; scrapbooking 106, 107
mulberry paper 29, 38

notelets 25
notepads 38, 48–9

origami 40, 50

paper, acid free 106, 107, 108; colouring 26; grain 6, 12; handmade 6, 7, 27, 110, 122–3; history 5; machine-made 6; storing 7, 107; weight 6
paper architecture 112, 116–17, 124
paper engineering 118
paper napkins 7; découpage 20, 36–7, 38
paper sculpture 112, 114–15
paper yarn 27, 28, 31, 110
parchment craft 6, 74, 76–85, 92–3, 125
patchwork 29, 92
photocopying templates 32
photographs 106–10
pictures and picture frames 39, 70–1, 74, 82–3, 131
pinching 66
place name cards 91
ply, paper napkins 36–37
pop-up 112, 118–24
pricking 38, 74, 76, 80, 86–7, 92 3
printed papers 6, 40
printing, computer 6, 76; rubber stamping 96–105
pull-outs 118, 119, 120–1, 124
punching 20, 22–5, 27, 38, 72, 73, 108–9, 124

quilling 6, 7, 38, 62–73
quilting 20, 28–31, 38

repetitive strain injury 10
ribbling 64, 65
rubber stamping 73, 94, 96–105, 110–11, 124

safety precautions 10
scoring 12, 45, 114, 116
scrapbooking 94, 106–9, 110
scraps 32, 34–5
scrolling 125; see also quilling
selling your work 11
sewing 26, 72, 73, 79, 85, 92, 110, 125, machine stitching 31, 86, 92; see also embroidery
shadow box 70–1
stamping see rubber stamping
stationery 16, 20, 25, 38, 48–9, 61, 74, 90–1, 98–9
stencils 9, 38, 39, 88–91, 107
storage 7, 9, 10

tags 20, 27, 37, 43, 61, 73, 105, 125
tea bag folding 40, 50–3, 60, 61, 73, 124
tearing 12–13, 110, 125
texture 6, 42, 64
3-D pieces 15, 38, 62, 64, 68–9, 74–93, 102–3, 111, 112 25
time management 10
tools and equipment 8–9; corner punch 22, 24; corner rounder 106; craft knife 9, 13; cutting mat 9; cutting templates 106, 108–9; embossing tools 76–7, 78, 88–9; felt-tip pens 81, 84–5, 93, 100, 102–3, 110, 124; fringing tool 64, 68, 70; guillotine 9, 107, 110; heat gun 104; inkpads 96, 100, 104; journaling pen 106, 109; lightbox 88–9; mapping pen 76, 84; needle and cork 28, 86–7; needle tools 80, 82–3, 86; oil pastels 81; paper trimmer 9, 107; punch wheel 13, 26, 82; quilling tool 64, 65; ribbler (crimper) 64, 65; rubber stamps 96, 97, 99; ruler 13; scissors 9; tweezers 33; watercolour pencils 81, 82–3, 100, 102–3, 111
tracing 76, 77

varnishing 32, 33, 35
vellum 60, 72, 76, 80
V-fold technique 119, 124

weaving 40, 42–3, 61
wedding stationary 16, 74, 90–1
wooden items, decorating 32–5, 36, 39, 64
workspace 10

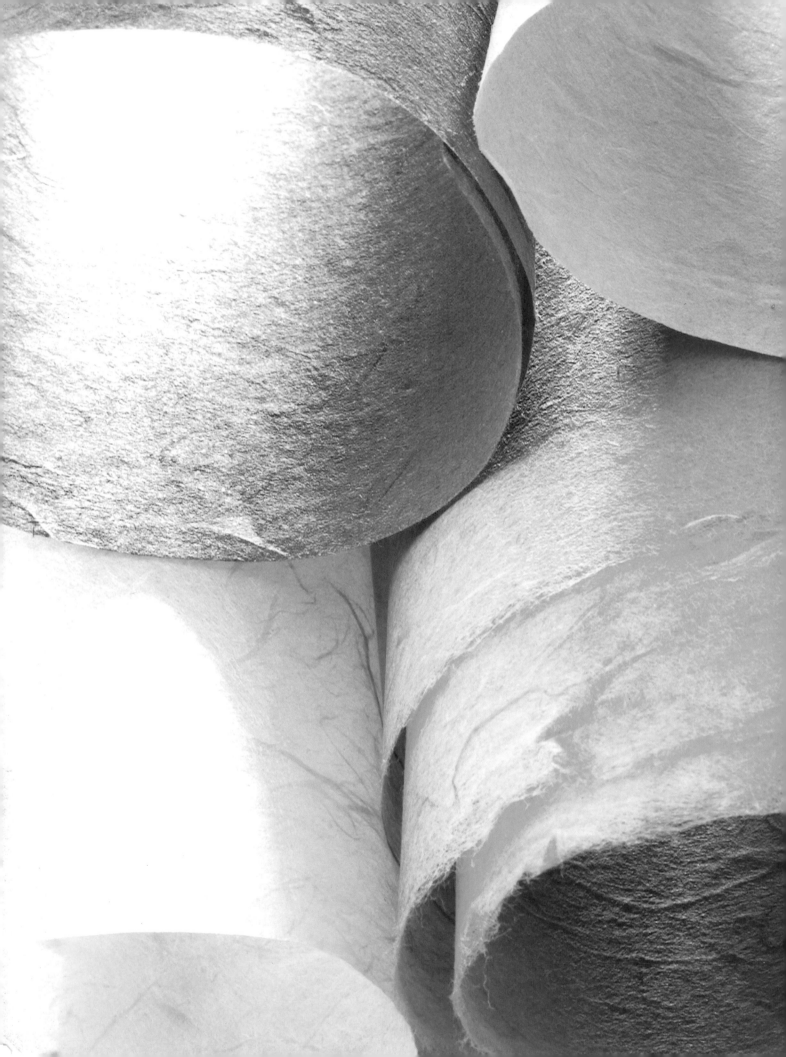